Crossroads Café
REPRODUCIBLE HANDOUTS

Elizabeth Minicz

HEINLE & HEINLE PUBLISHERS
I(T)P *An International Thomson Publishing Company*
Boston, Massachusetts 02116 U.S.A.

New York • London • Bonn • Boston • Detroit • Madrid • Melbourne • Mexico City • Paris •
Singapore • Tokyo • Toronto • Washington • Albany, NY • Belmont, CA • Cincinnati, OH

The publication of *Crossroads Café* was directed by the members of the Heinle & Heinle Secondary and Adult ESL Publishing Team.

Senior Editorial Director: Roseanne Mendoza
Senior Production Services Coordinator: Lisa McLaughlin
Market Development Director: Jonathan Boggs

Also participating in the publication of the program were:

Vice President and Publisher, ESL: Stanley Galek
Developmental Editor: Sally Conover
Managing Developmental Editor: Amy Lawler
Production Editor: Maryellen Killeen
Manufacturing Coordinator: Mary Beth Hennebury
Full Service Design and Production: PC&F, Inc.

ISBN: 0-8384-6615X

Heinle & Heinle is a division of International Thomson Publishing, Inc.

ACKNOWLEDGMENTS

With heartfelt thanks to the entire Crossroads Café team and especially Roseanne Mendoza, whose invitation to join the team delighted and challenged me; Sally Conover, whose expert editorial skills, ceaseless enthusiasm, constant encouragement, and infinite patience enabled me to complete an awesome task; and Lynn Savage, whose amazing abilities continue to inspire me.

TABLE OF CONTENTS

ABOUT THESE REPRODUCIBLE HANDOUTS

The Crossroads Café Worktexts are designed for independent learning or for pair or small group work with you, the partner. You can use the Crossroads Café Partner Guide and these reproducible handouts with the Worktexts to help learners improve their English. The four questions and answers that follow explain how to use the handouts with learners. Please notice that in this introduction, we refer to "learners," although we realize that many partners will be working with only one learner. The reproducible handouts also work very well in a one-to-one situation of that type.

1. WHAT IS THE PURPOSE OF THE REPRODUCIBLE HANDOUTS?

The **Handouts** link interaction activities to specific sections of the worktext. The chart below shows where the handouts are found in most episodes. However, there may be two **Handouts** for one worktext section when the language focus or the content is particularly challenging.

Worktext Section	Handout
YOUR NEW LANGUAGE	HANDOUT A
IN YOUR COMMUNITY	HANDOUT B
WHAT DO YOU THINK?	HANDOUT C
CULTURE CLIP	HANDOUT D

2. HOW DO I USE THE REPRODUCIBLE HANDOUTS?

The guidelines below help you to:

+ prepare the handouts for learners
+ ensure learners success in using the handouts
+ provide follow-up activities

Here are some ideas for preparing the handouts.

+ If possible, photocopy the handouts on card stock; they will be more durable and will last longer. If you store them in labeled envelopes, they can be used again and again.

+ Use the handouts after learners have completed worktext pages or watched the video. They should not be used to introduce or present new language—grammar and/or vocabulary. Learners will not be able to do the handouts successfully if the language and concepts are new to them.

+ Although some handouts tell learners to work in a small or in a large group, the handouts may be used by two learners working as a pair.

+ Handouts that need to be cut have dotted lines with a scissors icon. Whenever possible, have learners themselves cut and scramble the strips or cards used in the handouts. This will decrease your preparation time.

Here are some ideas for ensuring learner success.

- Explain the purpose of the handouts to learners. Stress that the handouts provide additional opportunities to practice the language and vocabulary of the videos and worktext and to exchange information and ideas with other learners.
- Model the activities so learners have a clear understanding of how to work with a partner or in a group.
- Review the directions orally. Ask learners if they have any questions.
- Monitor learners while they do the activities.
- Provide follow-up.

Here are some ideas for follow-up.

- Use cooperative learning structures such as *stand-up-and-share, best idea only,* and *teams share* to provide feedback. See the **Glossary** for definitions and examples.
- Post learners' work, when appropriate, on the walls for learners to read.
- Have pairs or small groups share role-plays with the rest of the class.
- Have learners reflect on their participation by asking themselves questions such as:

    "How well did I understand the activity?"
    "How much did I participate?"
    "Was I a good listener?"

- Have learners write about the activities in their journals.

3. WHAT IS THE PURPOSE OF THE ONE-PAGE SUMMARIES AT THE BEGINNING OF EACH UNIT?

There are two main purposes for the **Summaries**:

- to provide teachers and tutors with a summary of the video episode
- to provide a resource for additional activities for learners

Note: *The **Summaries** are written at a high-beginning/low-intermediate learner level.*

To see if the reading level of the summaries is appropriate for learners in your class, cover every seventh word and follow the directions in Option #4 on the next page. If learners identify less than 40% of the words correctly, don't use the summaries—they are too difficult.

4. HOW DO I USE THE SUMMARIES WITH LEARNERS?

Below are some options for using the summaries.

Option #1

- Make a photocopy of the summary for each learner.
- Have learners read it silently, as quickly as possible.
- Ask learners *yes/no, either/or,* and *wh- questions* about the content.
- Have learners read it again silently.

Option #2

- Have learners follow along while you read the summary aloud.
- As you read, change words (use synonyms or antonyms) and have learners correct you.

Option #3

- Make additional photocopies of the summary.
- Cut each copy into separate strips (one set for each learner or pair of learners).
- Scramble the strips and have learners put them in the correct order.

Option #4

- Retype the summary and delete selected words or cover selected words before you photocopy it. Make sure you leave the first and last lines intact.
- Have learners fill in the missing words.

Option #5

- Retype the summary and delete words, but don't leave spaces where the words were.
- Have learners read silently or follow along while you read aloud.
- Instruct learners to put a caret (^) every place a word is missing.

Victor Brashov is from Romania. He came to the United States 40 years ago. Now he is in his sixties and he is starting a new business. He is opening a restaurant.

It is a few days before the restaurant opens. Nothing is ready, but there are many people in the restaurant. Most of the people are workers. They are trying to get the restaurant ready to open.

One worker is Jamal. He is a handyman and a friend of Mr. Brashov. Jamal is from Egypt. He has a degree in engineering. He tries to fix Mr. Brashov's broken stove. This is a new kind of work for Jamal.

Another worker is a sign painter. He wants to paint the name of the restaurant on the sign. But Mr. Brashov does not have a name for his restaurant. This is just one of his many problems.

The chef is angry because the stove doesn't work. He quits. Now Mr. Brashov doesn't have a cook for his restaurant. He doesn't have any waiters or waitresses either.

Mr. Brashov puts an ad in the newspaper for waiters and waitresses. Several people come to apply for the jobs. Mr. Brashov doesn't like any of them.

Katherine Blake comes in. She was a waitress many years ago. She stayed home to take care of her children for ten years. Mr. Brashov likes Katherine, and he gives her a job.

Another woman comes to the restaurant. Her name is Rosa Rivera. She is from Mexico. Rosa also wants to be a waitress. But she can cook, so Mr. Brashov hires her to be the chef.

Now Mr. Brashov has employees. He can open his restaurant. But on opening day, the restaurant still does not have a name.

A teenager comes into the restaurant. His name is Henry. He is 17 years old and he is in high school. Today, there is no school. He needs directions to the post office.

Someone calls the restaurant and wants some food delivered. It is the first order. Mr. Brashov asks Henry to deliver the food.

Another person comes into the restaurant. He wants some coffee. His name is Jess Washington. Jess is retired. He worked for the post office. Jess likes to play chess. He plays with Jamal.

The sign painter is still in the restaurant. He wants to know the name of the restaurant. Everyone suggests names. Mr. Brashov does not like any of the names. Then Jess has an idea. He thinks Crossroads Café is a good name. Mr. Brashov likes it. Finally, the restaurant has a name!

ASK AND ANSWER

HANDOUT 1-A

Practice spelling your classmates' names and the names of their native countries. Ask the questions below. Write the answers on the lines.

QUESTIONS TO ASK: "What is your name?"   "How do you spell it?"
                   "Where are you from?"   "How do you spell it?"

EXAMPLE: A: What is your name?   B: My name is Jamal.
                   A: How do you spell it?   B: J-A-M-A-L
                   A: Could you repeat that?   B: Sure. J-A-M-A-L

NAME	NATIVE COUNTRY
1.	
2.	
3.	
4.	
5.	
6.	
7.	
8.	
9.	
10.	
11.	
12.	
13.	
14.	
15.	

CATEGORIES

HANDOUT 1-B

What do you talk about when you meet someone for the first time?

- ◆ Work with a partner or a small group.
- ◆ Cut and scramble the twelve cards and put them in a pile.
- ◆ One person picks up a question and reads it to the group.
- ◆ The group decides if the question is POLITE or IMPOLITE and puts it under the correct word.

✂ ---

POLITE QUESTIONS	IMPOLITE QUESTIONS
How do you like the weather?	How much do you weigh?
Are you married?	When are you going to have children?
Where do you live?	How much money do you make?
Where do you work?	Are you sick?
What kind of car do you have?	Why aren't you a U.S. citizen?
Where did you go to school?	How old are you?

INFORMATION GAP

HANDOUT 1-C

Sometimes people want to change jobs. But often they don't know how much money the new jobs pay. Fill in the chart below. Ask a partner about the jobs and salaries. Write the missing information in the blanks of the chart.

EXAMPLE: A: *What is the average salary of a computer engineer?*
B: *$70,000 a year.*

PARTNER A

JOB	SALARY	JOB	SALARY
computer engineer		high school teacher	$35,880
legal secretary	$30,712	optician	
baker		painter	$24,044
computer repairer	$30,212	pharmacist	
restaurant cook		hair stylist	$29,000
dental assistant	$20,592	licensed practical nurse	

 -

Sometimes people want to change jobs. But often they don't know how much money the new jobs pay. Fill in the chart below. Ask a partner about the jobs and salaries. Write the missing information in the blanks of the chart.

EXAMPLE: B: *What is the average salary of a high school teacher?*
A: *$35, 880 a year.*

PARTNER B

JOB	SALARY	JOB	SALARY
computer engineer	$70,000	high school teacher	
legal secretary		optician	$26,274
baker	$17,368	painter	
computer repairer		pharmacist	$49,608
restaurant cook	$25,000	hair stylist	
dental assistant		licensed practical nurse	$23,504

Crossroads Café   Opening Day

ROLE-PLAY

HANDOUT 1-D

Read these six newspaper ads.

- ♦ Work with a partner.
- ♦ Choose one ad that you both like.
- ♦ Decide who will be the employer and who will be the job applicant.
- ♦ Work together to write questions and answers about the job you chose. Then role-play a job interview.

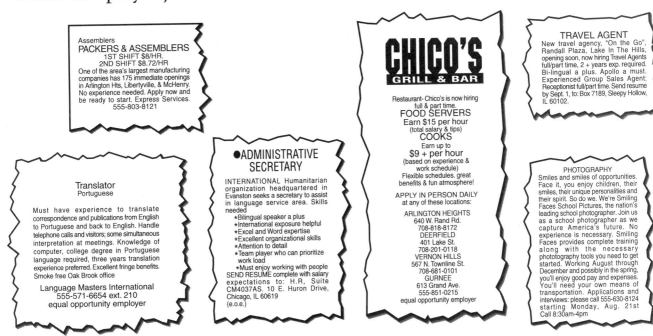

QUESTIONS	ANSWERS
1.	
2.	
3.	
4.	
5.	

Two unexpected visitors surprise the employees at Crossroads Café. The first unexpected visitor is Margaret Reilly. She's an inspector with the Department of Health and Safety. She is looking for health and safety problems in the café.

The second unexpected visitor is Henry's uncle. He and his friend are at Crossroads Café for a take-out order. Henry doesn't want his uncle to see him because his parents don't know about his job.

Henry tries to hide from his uncle. Rosa asks Henry, "What's going on?" Henry tells her, "My parents don't know I am working here." Rosa wants Henry to tell Mr. Brashov about this, but Henry is afraid to tell him.

Ms. Reilly, the inspector, makes the employees nervous. She walks around and writes on a clipboard. She is not very friendly. She wants to inspect everything: Mr. Brashov's office, the bathrooms, and the kitchen. She has a lot of questions. She wants someone to show her around the café and answer questions. Jamal shows her around the café.

Henry tells Mr. Brashov, "I have something important to talk to you about." But Mr. Brashov does not understand. He tells Henry not to worry. He is doing a good job.

When Henry gets home, there is a birthday party at his house. It is his brother's 13th birthday. Henry's uncle comes to the party. Mr. and Mrs. Chang find out about Henry's job. They are very angry. Henry's parents want him to quit his job at Crossroads Café. They don't think Henry can do schoolwork, practice the violin, and work.

At Crossroads Café, Jamal helps Ms. Reilly. He shows her around the restaurant and answers her questions. Ms. Reilly finds some toxic chemicals. She says they are dangerous to have around food. She gives Mr. Brashov some forms to fill out. Mr. Brashov is worried about the inspection.

Mr. and Mrs. Chang come to Crossroads Café. Mr. Brashov finally learns about Henry's problem. Now he finds out about Henry's big lie. Henry's parents did not give him permission to work. They did not sign the work permission form from Henry's school. Someone else signed it! Now Mr. Brashov is angry, too.

Ms. Reilly is still in the café. She talks to Katherine and Rosa. Katherine has a headache after she talks to Ms. Reilly. But Rosa is happy to talk to Ms. Reilly. She loves to show people her kitchen. She gets along very well with Ms. Reilly.

Then everyone hears a scream. It's Ms. Reilly. Henry's violin case was in the kitchen. Ms. Reilly fell over it. She complains to Mr. Brashov. Now Mr. Brashov is really worried about the inspection.

Mr. and Mrs. Chang are surprised to see Henry's violin case. They are happy because Henry is practicing his violin. They tell him, "If you keep up with your school work and violin lessons, you can keep your job." They will decide in a few weeks.

Two weeks pass. Mr. Brashov is opening the mail. It's good news. First there is a report from Ms. Reilly. Crossroads Café passed the inspection. There is also a letter from Mr. and Mrs. Chang. They signed Henry's work form. He can keep his job!

INTERVIEW

HANDOUT 2-A

Ms. Reilly comes to inspect Crossroads Café for health and safety problems. Think about your home. Is it safe? Do the safety check below.

- Answer the questions about your home.
- Interview a partner about his or her home. Add two questions to the chart.
- Compare your answers. Offer suggestions to make your partner's home safer.
- Share your answers with another pair.

EXAMPLE: Q: *Do you use a lot of extension cords?*
A: *No, I don't. How about you?*
Q: *Yes, I do.*

	MY HOME		MY PARTNER'S	
	YES	NO	YES	NO
Do you avoid using a lot of extension cords?				
Is medicine stored away from children?				
Are cleaning supplies away from food?				
Do you have smoke detectors?				
Do you have a carbon monoxide detector?				
Do you keep things off the floor?				
Do you keep electrical appliances away from water?				
Do you replace loose or frayed cords on any electrical appliances?				
Do you keep matches and lighters away from children?				

DIALOGUE

HANDOUT 2-B

Henry's uncle doesn't know Henry has a job. Rosa finds out about Henry's problem.

- ◆ Work with a partner.
- ◆ Cut, scramble, and read the dialogue cards below.
- ◆ While you watch the video clip, put Rosa and Henry's conversation in order.
- ◆ Share with another pair. Is the order of the cards the same?

✂ -

ROSA: Henry, what's going on?
HENRY: Well, my parents don't exactly know I'm working here.
ROSA: Oh Henry . . .
HENRY: What's the big deal? I mean lots of kids do it. School in the morning. Work in the afternoon.
ROSA: The big deal is you didn't tell your parents. What's Mr. Brashov going to say?
HENRY: Maybe he'll never find out.
ROSA: Oh yes he will.
HENRY: How can you be so sure?
ROSA: Because you're going to tell him.
HENRY: I am?
ROSA: Either you are . . . or I am.

Reproducible Handouts   9

CATEGORIES

HANDOUT 2-C

There are different kinds of lies. White lies are not serious. People usually tell white lies because they don't want to hurt someone's feelings. Black lies are very serious. They can cause big problems.

- ◆ Work with a partner.
- ◆ Cut, scramble, and read the lies on the cards.
- ◆ Write two more lies on the blank cards.
- ◆ Sort cards into two piles: one for white lies and the other for black lies.
- ◆ Share with the class.

✂ -

You don't want to go to a friend's party, so you say you're sick.	A coworker asks to borrow $20.00 until pay day. You don't like to lend money, so you say you don't have any.
The phone rings and you don't feel like talking to anyone. You tell your husband to say you aren't home.	Your friend has a new haircut. You don't like it, but you say it looks nice.
Your boss asks you to work overtime. You say your child is sick and have to take her to the doctor.	Your family is visiting from your country. You want to be with them so you call in sick to work.
You found a gold ring in the restroom. It fits so you keep it. Someone asks if you saw a ring in the restroom and you say no.	You overslept and you are late to work. You tell your boss you are late because you had a car accident.
Your neighbor asks you to watch her child. You don't like the child. You say you have plans.	You are angry at your friend. She asks what's wrong. You say, "Nothing."
Your classmate asks for a ride home after school. It is out of your way. You say you have a doctor's appointment after class.	A friend asks to borrow your car. You don't like to loan things. You say the brakes aren't working.
At a job interview, you say you have more education than you really do.	Someone asks you for directions to the post office. You are in a hurry so you say you don't know.

COMPARE CULTURES

HANDOUT 2-D

Henry's parents did not want him to work. What do you think? Should teenagers work? Do they work in your country?

- ♦ Answer the questions below.
- ♦ Check the boxes and write in the spaces below the questions.
- ♦ Share your answers with a partner.

	U.S.		MY COUNTRY	
	YES	NO	YES	NO
Do children under age 14 work? What kinds of jobs do they have?				
Do teenagers over age 14 work? What kinds of jobs do they have?				
Are working children protected by laws? If so, what are some?				
Are there any jobs children cannot do? If so, what are these jobs?				
Do parents have to give permission for children under 16 to work?				
Do you think teenagers should work? Why or why not?				
Do you think children under 14 should work? Why or why not?				
Do schools help children learn about different kinds of jobs?				

UNIT 3   WORLDS APART

Lunch hour is almost over at Crossroads Café. Two women, Mrs. Gilroy and her friend want to order lunch. Mrs. Gilroy suggests the special, Monterey Chicken.

The two women see Mr. Brashov. Mr. Brashov looks very tired. He is not sleeping well at night. When he comes to work, he is tired and he forgets things.

Rosa enters the café with her friend Miguel. She introduces him to Mr. Brashov and the other employees. Miguel is from Rosa's hometown, Puebla, Mexico. Miguel is an architect, and he is on his way to a conference.

Rosa takes Miguel to her apartment. She wants to introduce Miguel to her roommate, Carrie. But Carrie is not home. Miguel gives Rosa a necklace. The necklace belonged to his mother and his grandmother.

Miguel wants to marry Rosa. He wants her to return to Mexico to live. Rosa tells Miguel about her dreams. She is taking business classes because she wants to have her own restaurant someday. He says, "You can open a restaurant in Puebla, Rosa. I will help you."

When Miguel leaves her apartment, Rosa cannot sleep. She stays up late and thinks about her restaurant. She draws plans for the building, and she thinks about the menu.

The next day, Rosa tells Miguel about her ideas for her restaurant. Rosa wants to have the kitchen in the middle of the restaurant so people can watch her cook. She also wants to have international food on the menu. Miguel says, "You forget, Rosita. This is Puebla, Mexico. The people in Mexico will not come to your restaurant." This makes Rosa very sad.

At the café, Mr. Brashov's brother Nicolae calls. He will send Mr. Brashov something to help him sleep. It is almost lunch time, but Mr. Brashov leaves the café. He goes to the bank to sign loan papers.

Then the phone rings. It is for Katherine. Her daughter was hurt at school. Katherine must go to the hospital. When Katherine leaves, there is no waitress.

A group of women enter the café. They made a lunch reservation with Mr. Brashov, but he forgot to tell Rosa. Because Mr. Brashov and Katherine are not at the café, Rosa must do their jobs. She greets the customers and takes their food orders. Henry helps her.

The women want to eat Rosa's special chicken recipe, but it's not on the menu today. Rosa likes to try out new recipes. She persuades them to try Chicken San Joaquin, and they love it.

Rosa does not want to go back to Mexico. She wants to live in the United States. The U.S. is her home now. Miguel does not understand this. Rosa decides not to marry Miguel.

The next day a package comes from Nicolae in Romania. He knows why Victor cannot sleep, so he sends Victor a special pillow. The pillow belonged to Mr. Brashov when he was a boy.

Then Victor remembers. It is his 40th wedding anniversary, and he misses his dead wife. Now, he can sleep again.

Reproducible Handouts

SAME AND DIFFERENT

HANDOUT 3-A

Work with a partner. One person is **A** and the other is **B**. Work together to complete the grid below.

♦ In the *top left-hand box*, write **four** things you both want to do.
♦ In the *top right-hand box* write **four** things **A** wants to do but **B** doesn't want to do.
♦ In the *bottom left-hand box*, write **four** things **B** wants to do, but **A** doesn't want to do.
♦ In the *bottom right-hand box* write **four** things neither of you want to do.

BOTH A AND B	ONLY A
ONLY B	**NEITHER A NOR B**

HANDOUT 3-B

You and some friends are at an Italian restaurant for lunch. Together you have only $20. Look at the menu below.

- ◆ One person in your group is the waiter or waitress.
- ◆ Decide what you want to eat. Make sure the bill comes to $20.00 or less. Don't forget tax and tip.
- ◆ Give your order to the waiter or waitress.
- ◆ The waiter or waitress writes down the order and adds up the bill.
- ◆ Compare the two amounts. Are they the same or different? Why or why not?

HOMEMADE PASTA SPECIALTIES

SPAGHETTI or MOSTACCIOLI with meat sauce	$3.40
LASAGNA	$5.15
STUFFED SHELLS	$5.15

HOUSE SPECIALTIES

CHICKEN CACCIATORE	$7.00
EGGPLANT PARMIGIANA	$6.45
21-PIECE SHRIMP DINNER	$6.00

SANDWICHES

SUBMARINE	$3.15
BAR-B-Q BEEF	$3.55
ITALIAN ROAST BEEF	$3.40
FISH FILET	$2.60
PEPPER & EGG	$2.35
STEAK	$4.00
HOT DOG & FRIES	$1.95

SIDE ORDERS

SALAD	$1.30	MINESTRONE SOUP	$1.60
CHEESE STICKS	$2.65	CHICKEN WINGS (6)	$2.75
FRENCH FRIES	$1.30	GARLIC BREAD	$1.30

BEVERAGES

SOFT DRINKS (per can)	$.60	TEA OR COFFEE	$.85

COMPARE AND SHARE

HANDOUT 3-C

When Rosa tells Miguel about her restaurant plans, he says, "Puebla, Mexico is not the United States of America." Think about restaurants in your native country and the United States. What is the same? What is different?

- ◆ Answer the questions below. Check the boxes, and write in the spaces below the questions.
- ◆ Think of two more questions and write them in the blanks.
- ◆ Share your answers with a partner.

	U.S.			MY COUNTRY		
	YES	NO		YES	NO	
1. Do people eat in restaurants a lot?			How often?			How often?
2. Do people like to eat food from other countries?			What?			What?
3. Do parents take their children to restaurants?			When? What kind?			When? What kind?
4. Do people tip in restaurants?			How much?			How much?
5. Do you like to eat in restaurants?			Why or why not?			Why or why not?
6. Do you have a favorite food to eat in restaurants?			What is it?			What is it?
7. Is one kind of restaurant more popular than others?			What kind?			What kind?
8.						
9.						

THINK AND SPEAK

HANDOUT 3-D

Think about your life in the United States. How is it the same as and different from your native country?

- ◆ Read the topics below.
- ◆ Add two more topics on the blank cards.
- ◆ Cut out the cards, shuffle them, and put them face down in a pile.
- ◆ Take turns: pick a card from the pile and say three sentences about the topic.

✂ -

Food	Travel
Families	Housing
Children	Friends
Work	Marriage
Education	Gifts

UNIT 4   WHO'S THE BOSS?

Jamal was an engineer in Egypt. He designed bridges and highways. Now he is a handyman at Crossroads Café. Jamal is trying to fix the café's alarm system, but he is having a few problems.

Mr. Brashov is waiting for a phone call from the *Restaurant News*. He wants the newspaper to write about Crossroads Café so it will have more business.

Jamal asks to go home early. He and his wife, Jihan, are going out in the evening. They're going to a special reception for an important man from Egypt. The man used to be Jamal's boss. Mr. Brashov says, "Of course you can leave early for such a special occasion."

Jess is in the café. He doesn't hear Katherine when she talks to him. Mr. Brashov decides to talk to Jess about his hearing problem. But Jess gets angry and leaves the café.

That night at the reception, Jamal meets some old friends from Egypt. His friends talk about their jobs, and they want to know about Jamal's job. Jamal says, "I'm in the restaurant business now." He doesn't say, " I am a handyman." Jamal is embarrassed because he doesn't have a professional job anymore.

The next day, someone from the *Restaurant News* calls Crossroads Café. A reporter is coming to interview Mr. Brashov. But he doesn't know when the reporter will come. Mr. Brashov decides to go to the bank.

While Mr. Brashov is at the bank, Jamal's friends from Egypt come to the café. They want to surprise Jamal. But he is not happy to see his friends because they think he's the boss.

Jamal decides to act like the boss. That makes Katherine and Rosa angry. They don't know about Jamal's friends in the café. Finally, Jamal tells Rosa and Katherine his problem. They decide to help Jamal, and they pretend he is the boss.

But then Mr. Brashov comes back from the bank. He asks Jamal, "How is the burglar alarm coming?" Jamal tells Mr. Brashov to fix it right away. Mr. Brashov is very surprised. He asks, "Who is the handyman around here?" And Jamal says, "You are?"

Then Katherine takes Mr. Brashov into the kitchen. She tells him about Jamal's problem. Now Mr. Brashov also pretends Jamal is the boss. He apologizes to him.

Jess comes into the café. His ears were cleaned and now he can hear. But he is confused because Mr. Brashov calls Jamal "boss."

Henry comes to work. He doesn't know Jamal is the "boss." He is confused, too. Then, a man in the café stands up. He is from the *Restaurant News,* and he wants to interview the owner. Jamal has to tell his friends the truth about his job.

Jamal didn't need to lie to his friends. They admire Jamal because he left everything in Egypt to come to the United States. They don't care if Jamal is a handyman or a restaurant owner. They are his friends.

The next day Jess brings a newspaper into the café. There is an article about Crossroads Café. The title is "Who's the Boss?".

ROLE-PLAY

HANDOUT 4-A

People say, "I'm sorry" or "Sorry" when they want to apologize.

♦ Work with a partner.
♦ Each person should write one role-play situation on a blank card.
♦ Scramble the cards and put them face down in a pile.
♦ Take turns turning over the cards and role-playing the situations.
♦ Each pair shares one role-play with the rest of the class.

You are standing in a line and you step on someone's toe.	You borrowed a book from a friend. You are returning it three months later.
You are introduced to someone and you forget the person's name.	You're in the grocery store and you just discovered you have another customer's cart.
You didn't hear what your friend said.	You were very busy after dinner and didn't have time to return a phone call from your friend.
Your spouse or partner asks if you mailed the bills. You didn't.	You lost your English book and have to ask your teacher for another one.
Your spouse or partner asks if you put gas in the car. You forgot.	You didn't give a coworker an important phone message.
You arrive 20 minutes late for your dentist appointment.	You borrowed a CD from your friend. You lost it.

DIALOGUE

HANDOUT 4-B

Mr. Brashov is upset. He wants the *Restaurant News* to write about Crossroads Café.

♦ Work with a partner.
♦ Cut, scramble, and read the dialogue cards below.
♦ While you watch the video, put the conversation in order.
♦ Share with another pair. Is the order of the cards the same?

✂ -

MR. BRASHOV: Katherine, has anyone called me from the *Restaurant News?*

KATHERINE: Not since you asked me an hour ago.

MR. BRASHOV: Maybe they sent a letter?

KATHERINE: I gave you all the mail this morning.

JESS: Victor, you look upset. What's the problem?

MR. BRASHOV: It's this newspaper. I'm trying to get them to come to Crossroads Café.

JESS: The *Restaurant News?*

MR. BRASHOV: They list all the restaurants in town and interview the owners. It would be a good way to attract new customers.

HENRY: We should be in there. Why don't you call them?

MR. BRASHOV: I already have and now I'm waiting for an answer.

INFORMATION GAP

HANDOUT 4-C

You and a friend are going out to eat to celebrate your new job.
- ♦ Look at the ad below for the Japanese Hibachi House.
- ♦ Ask a partner questions about the missing information in your ad.

  EXAMPLE: Q: *What kind of super special is it?*
             A: *Dinner.*

- ♦ Write the information in the blanks.

SUPER _____ SPECIAL
Large Shrimp & Chicken with French Garlic Sauce $ _____ (for two people)
Includes _____ shrimp, soup, salad, and vegetables.

Offer good thru _____ . Present coupon before dinner.

LOBSTER SPECIAL
Steak and Lobster $22.95

SPECIALS
Teri Yaki _____ . . . . $10.75   Hibachi Steak. $12.75
Shrimp & Scallops. . . . . _____   _____ $17.75

CALL 893-3377 FOR _____

You and a friend are going out to eat to celebrate your new job.
- ♦ Look at the ad below for the Japanese Hibachi House.
- ♦ Ask a partner questions about the missing information in your ad.

  EXAMPLE: Q: *How many people is the $22.00 special for?*
             A: *Two.*

- ♦ Write the information in the blanks.

SUPER DINNER SPECIAL
Large Shrimp & Chicken with _____ Garlic Sauce $22.00 (for _____ people)
Includes appetizers, shrimp, soup, salad, and _____ .

Offer good thru 1/31. Present coupon before _____ .

LOBSTER SPECIAL
Steak and Lobster . . . . $ _____

SPECIALS
Teri Yaki Chicken. . . . . $ _____   _____ Steak. $12.75
Shrimp & Scallops. . . . . $16.95   Shrimp & Scallops. . . . . $ _____

CALL _____ FOR SUPER DINNER SPECIAL

Crossroads Café   Who's the Boss?

SOLVE THE PROBLEM

HANDOUT 4-D

Jamal is trained as an engineer. Now he is the handyman at Crossroads Café.

- ◆ Work with a partner.
- ◆ Write the information for Jamal in the boxes below.
- ◆ Think about your job or a friend's job.
- ◆ Make another chart for yourself.

Good things about present job	Bad things about present job
Skills and knowledge developed	Things to do to change situation

Katherine lost her keys. The other employees help her look for them. Finally, Mr. Brashov finds the keys. They were next to the coffee machine.

A police officer is at Carol and Jess Washington's house. They are reporting a burglary. Someone robbed their house. It is a mess. The burglar stole an old TV, a VCR, and a toaster oven. The burglar also broke Jess's wooden airplane.

Jess comes into Crossroads Café. Several people are eating lunch. A woman is asking questions about the fish. Then the door to the café opens. Three young boys come running in the door. They are shouting and throwing a football. When Mr. Brashov tells them to stop, they are rude to him. The customers in the café do not like this, and they walk out.

One of the young boys is Katherine's son, David. Katherine is very angry. Katherine sees David's watch. "Where did you get it?" she asks. David says, "I found it at school." Katherine knows this is a lie. The counselor at David's school called her. David did not go to school this week.

The boys leave the café. Katherine argues with David. A few minutes later, David runs out of the café. Katherine is very worried about David. It is hard for Katherine to be both a mother and a father to David.

A salesperson from "A to Z Security" is at the Washington's house. He is trying to sell Jess and Carol a security system. It is very expensive, so Jess and Carol do not buy it.

David is at Crossroads Café again. This time he is doing homework in the utility room. He is not happy to be there. He throws his books and papers on the floor. Then he picks up a hammer and hits some wood.

Jess comes into the room. He sees David with the hammer. "Does that hammer belong to you?" Jess asks David. David says to Jess, "You sound like a cop."

Jess and David talk. They talk about their fathers. When Jess was 10 years old, his father went away. He left Jess a note and a wooden airplane. The burglar broke it.

David's parents are divorced. He used to build things with his father. Now he never sees him. David's feelings are very hurt.

Jess worries about safety all of the time. He reads newspaper stories about crime. He asks Jamal to hook up an alarm system. It doesn't work. Jess doesn't want Carol to go out alone at night. Carol thinks Jess worries too much. She invites people in the neighborhood to her house to talk about safety. Many people come to the meeting.

Katherine is waiting for David to come to the café after school. He is late, and she is not happy. Finally, David comes. He was in the wood shop at school. He has a friend with a broken airplane, and David wants to fix it. Jess is the friend.

The employees think of other things for David to make. They suggest a coat rack and a sign for Rosa's specials. But Rosa has the best idea. She suggests a key holder for Katherine.

HANDOUT 5-A

Katherine lost her keys. The employees at Crossroads Café help her look for them.

- ◆ Work with a partner.
- ◆ Cut, scramble, and read the dialogue cards below.
- ◆ While you watch the video, put the conversation in order.
- ◆ Share with another pair. Is the order of the cards the same?

✂ -

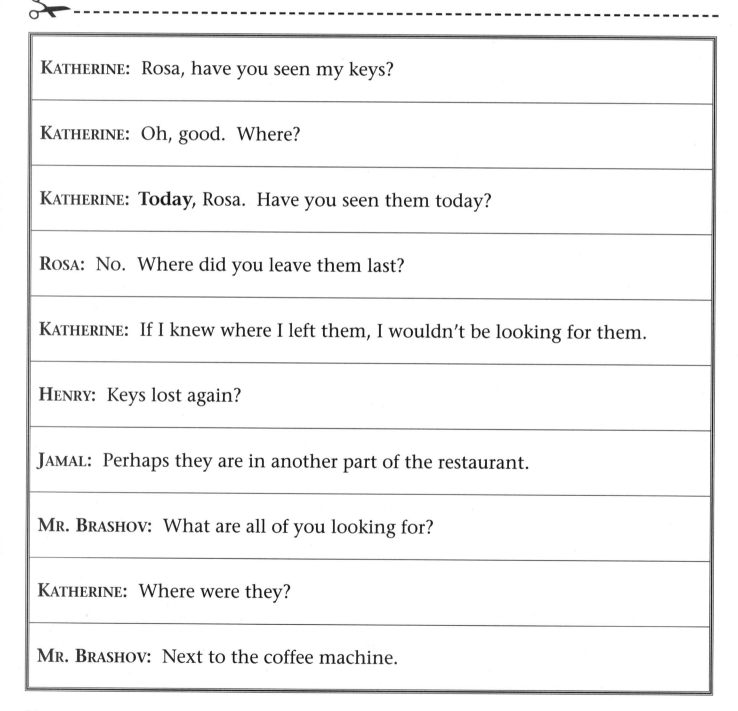

KATHERINE: Rosa, have you seen my keys?

KATHERINE: Oh, good. Where?

KATHERINE: **Today**, Rosa. Have you seen them today?

ROSA: No. Where did you leave them last?

KATHERINE: If I knew where I left them, I wouldn't be looking for them.

HENRY: Keys lost again?

JAMAL: Perhaps they are in another part of the restaurant.

MR. BRASHOV: What are all of you looking for?

KATHERINE: Where were they?

MR. BRASHOV: Next to the coffee machine.

SCRAMBLED SENTENCES

HANDOUT 5-B

You are going on vacation. The scrambled sentences below tell you what to do before you leave.

- ♦ Work with a partner.
- ♦ Put the words of the scrambled sentences in the correct order.
- ♦ Read the sentences. Add capital letters and periods.
- ♦ Then add two more things to do.
- ♦ Share your things to do with the rest of the class.

✂ -

all	lock	doors

lock	close	windows	and	them	the

mail	stop	the

to	neighbor	house	watch
a	your	ask	

oven	make	and	sure
the	off	are	stove

drapes	curtains	close	or	the

newspapers	stop	the

timers	lights	for	set	the

SOLVE THE PROBLEM

HANDOUT 5-C

Katherine has problems with her son. He is not going to school. He is rude to his mother, and his friends are rude to Mr. Brashov.

♦ Work with a partner or a small group.
♦ Read the problems below.
♦ Decide how to solve the problems.
♦ Write one more problem. Give it to another pair or group to solve.
♦ Share your solutions with the rest of the class.

✂ -

PROBLEM #1   You are the parents of a 13-year-old boy. Your son used to be a good student. Now he is failing two classes, and he has low grades in the others. You don't know your son's new friends. Your son is rude to you and he doesn't want to spend time with the family.
What can you do to help your son?

PROBLEM #2   Your daughter is 10 years old. She cries everyday when she comes home from school. Some children in her class yell at her and call her names. Sometimes they throw things at her.
What can you do to help her?

PROBLEM #3   It's 6 o'clock in the morning. You go outside to get the newspaper. You are very upset. Somebody threw eggs at your house. There is toilet paper and garbage all over. Your car has four flat tires and a window is broken.
What can you do?

PROBLEM #4   It is late at night. Everyone in your family is sleeping. You wake up. You think you hear noises. It sounds like breaking glass. Then you hear voices.
What can you do?

PROBLEM # 5

INTERVIEW

HANDOUT 5-D

There was a burglary at Carol and Jess Washington's house. Have you ever been a victim of a crime?

- ♦ Interview a partner about crime.
- ♦ Write your partner's answers in the spaces.
- ♦ Share your interview with the rest of the class.

NAME: INTERVIEWER:
1. Have you ever been a victim of a crime or seen a crime?
2. What was the crime?
3. What did you do?
4. What happened?
5. How did you feel?
6. Do you feel safe in your home?
7. Do you feel safe in your neighborhood?
8. Do you go out at night?
9. What do you do to be safe?
10. Did you feel safe in your native country? Why or why not?

Mr. Brashov is sitting at a table in the café. He is not working in his office because Jamal is fixing the air conditioner. Mr. Brashov is unhappy. He likes owning a business, but he hates the paperwork.

Henry is late for work and everyone is waiting for him. Katherine has to pick up her children from school. Rosa has to go to the library before her business class. Mr. Brashov tells them to go. Finally, Henry comes. He was buying tickets for a rock concert.

Jess has a suggestion for Mr. Brashov. His son has a friend from school, Emery Bradford. Emery can help organize Mr. Brashov's paperwork. Jess gives Emery's business card to Mr. Brashov and tells him to call Emery. Mr. Brashov is not interested.

The air conditioner comes on. Unfortunately, it blows Mr. Brashov's paperwork on the floor. Then he takes Emery Bradford's business card from Jess.

Rosa is at her business management class. The teacher has a special project for the class. Rosa and Armando, another student, will be managers of a mail room. They have to organize the other students so they can wrap a package to send.

Armando's team works well together. He encourages them to do a good job. Rosa's team does not work well together. She tells them what to do and tries to make them work faster. Rosa takes over. Her team did not do well, and she feels like a failure.

Emery is at Crossroads Café. He organizes Mr. Brashov's paperwork and helps him make a schedule for paying bills. He walks around with a clipboard and timer. He watches the employees and makes notes. Emery looks for ways to save time. He tells Mr. Brashov, "Time is money."

Emery makes many changes at Crossroads Café. The employees work faster and wear uniforms now. Mr. Brashov is wearing a white shirt and bow tie.

Emery announces a contest. Mr. Brashov will give $100 to the most efficient employee. But Mr. Brashov is not happy. He likes to talk to the customers. Emery does not like this. If Mr. Brashov talks to the customers, they sit at the tables too long. Emery wants customers to eat quickly and leave, so there are tables for more customers.

Finally Emery announces the winner of the contest. Katherine hopes to be the winner. But she is not. It is Rosa. Then Rosa surprises everyone. She does not accept the prize. She says, "The award does not belong just to me. It belongs to all of us." Rosa understands teamwork now.

Mr. Brashov disagrees. He thinks Emery should win the award. He gives Emery the trophy and the check and says good-bye. He takes off his tie and throws it in the air.

Several days later, everything is back to normal at Crossroads Café. Jamal makes an announcement. The air conditioner is fixed. He turns it on, and it blows Mr. Brashov's papers all over the room.

ROLE PLAY

HANDOUT 6-A

Here are three different ways to make suggestions.

Why don't you have some lunch?
Maybe you should have some lunch.
How about having some lunch?

♦ Work with a partner.
♦ Write suggestions and answers for the people below. Use the expressions shown above.
♦ Take turns role-playing the suggestions.
♦ Add another role-play situation.

✂ -

Father:
Child:
Husband:
Wife:
Brother:
Sister:
Grandparent:
Grandchild:
Sales Clerk:
Customer:
Neighbor:
Neighbor:
Supervisor:
Employee:

MIX AND MATCH

HANDOUT 6-B

- ◆ Cut the cards and put them in two piles: problems and solutions.
- ◆ Scramble each pile: Half of the learners take a problem card and the other half take a suggestion card.
- ◆ Walk around the room and ask questions to match the problems and suggestions.
- ◆ When you find a match, sit down.

PROBLEMS	SOLUTIONS
I'm hot.	Why don't you open a window?
I'm cold.	Why don't you put on a sweater?
I'm bored.	Why don't you rent a video?
My neighbors play loud music every night.	Why don't you ask them to turn the volume down?
I'd like something to drink.	How about a glass of iced tea?
My car is making funny noises.	Maybe you should take it to a mechanic.
I'd like to read a good book.	How about *Jurassic Park?*
I need to buy a new car.	How about a Ford Mustang?
My boss doesn't like me.	Maybe you should look for a new job.
I don't make enough money.	Maybe you should ask for a raise.

INFORMATION GAP

HANDOUT 6-C

Rosa takes the bus to her class. Look at this bus schedule with a partner.

♦ Ask and answer questions to find the missing information.

    EXAMPLE: *A: What time is the first stop at Gladstone?*
                    B: 5:38

♦ Write the information in the blanks.

PARTNER A

GLADSTONE	STEVENSON	PRESIDENT	GLEN FALLS APARTMENTS	TRAIN STATION
	5:42		5:57	6:13
5:58		6:12		6:35
	6:34			
NO STOP			7:12	
NO STOP	7:22	7:30		7:48
NO STOP		7:55	8:02	

 -

Rosa takes the bus to her class. Look at this bus schedule with a partner.

♦ Ask and answer questions to find the missing information.

    EXAMPLE: *B: What time is the first stop at Stevenson?*
                    A: 5:42

♦ Write the information in the blanks.

PARTNER B

GLADSTONE	STEVENSON	PRESIDENT	GLEN FALLS APARTMENTS	TRAIN STATION
5:38		5:50		
	6:04		6:19	
6:20		6:42	6:49	7:00
NO STOP	6:57	7:05		7:23
NO STOP			7:37	
NO STOP	7:47			8:13

SOLVE THE PROBLEM

HANDOUT 6-D

People often say, "I never seem to have enough time to do everything I want to do."

- ♦ Make a list of 5–7 daily activities.
- ♦ Estimate how much time you spend on each activity.
- ♦ Share your list with a partner.
- ♦ Your partner reads the list and makes suggestions to save time.
- ♦ Decide which suggestions you will follow.
- ♦ Share your time-saving ideas with the rest of the class.

DAILY ACTIVITIES	TIME SPENT
1.	
2.	
3.	
4.	
5.	
6.	
7.	

SUGGESTIONS FOR SAVING TIME:

1.
2.
3.
4.
5.
6.
7.

It is almost closing time at Crossroads Café. Everyone is waiting for Mr. Brashov and his brother Nicolae. Nicolae is coming from Romania. He was the manager of a tourist hotel on the Black Sea. Now he will be Mr. Brashov's new partner.

The door opens and everyone welcomes Nicolae. He is younger and thinner than Mr. Brashov. He also speaks English very well.

Nicolae recognizes the employees at Crossroads Café because Victor sent him pictures. But Nicolae doesn't know Jess. When Victor introduces Jess to Nicolae, Victor says, "Meet Crossroads Café's best customer."

When everyone leaves, Victor and Nicolae are alone. They talk and eat a snack. Nicolae wants to speak Romanian. Victor doesn't. His brother does not understand why Victor isn't interested in Romania.

The café is open. Nicolae is trying to learn about the business. First he drops plates when he serves customers. Then he uses a cart. He helps Jamal. He teaches Rosa a new recipe. He figures out how to save money, and he plays chess with Jess. He even wants to help Henry with deliveries.

Nicolae says, "We used to ride bicycles all the time. Why stop now?" Victor taught him to ride a bicycle when he was a boy. He wants to ride a bicycle again with his brother. Victor has no time. Work at the café comes first.

Victor has the flu. Nicolae runs the restaurant for him. He changes the menu, redecorates, and hires Romanian musicians. Crossroads Café looks like a Romanian restaurant.

When Victor returns to the café, he is very angry. He tells the musicians to go. He argues with Nicolae. Nicolae is angry, too. He says to Victor, "You are ashamed of our customs, our language." Nicolae leaves the café.

Nicolae is at a mall. He is buying something, and he sees one of the Romanian musicians. Nicolae tries to follow him, but there are too many people.

Nicolae is walking in the mall. He sees the musician again. Then Nicolae loses his wallet. He takes candy from a little girl, but he doesn't pay for it. The little girl tells a police officer. Nicolae sees them talking. He looks for his wallet, but he cannot find it. He gives the candy to the police officer and runs away.

Nicolae is on the street again. A woman asks him for money and he gives her everything in his pocket. Then Nicolae hears some music. He follows the music and climbs some stairs. He is in a Romanian cabaret. Romanian music is playing. Everyone from Crossroads Café is there, but they do not see Nicolae or speak to him. They ignore him. Finally a man speaks to Nicolae in Romanian. Nicolae asks, "Where am I?" The man says, "You are home."

Mr. Brashov is very sad. Nicolae is at the airport. He is going back to Romania. Nicolae gave Victor a package before he left. Mr. Brashov opens it. It is a beautiful music box.

A man comes into the café. He found Nicolae's wallet. Victor calls the airport to tell Nicolae. He also says, "I know you need to go. I want to visit you soon. We can ride bicycles, too."

    Reproducible Handouts   **37**

MATCH

HANDOUT 7-A

Jamal repairs many things at Crossroads Café. Last week he repaired the stove.
He has repaired the toaster several times. As long as Jamal works at Crossroads
Café, he will repair things.

- ♦ Work with a partner or small group.
- ♦ Cut and scramble the cards. Put them face down in four columns and seven rows.
- ♦ Take turns. One person turns over two cards. If the cards have the same verb, that person keeps the cards.
- ♦ If the cards don't match, the person puts them face down again.
- ♦ When all of the cards have matched, each person dictates a sentence for each verb card he or she has.
- ♦ Share your sentences with another pair or group.

✂ -

have	had	bring	brought
run	run	teach	taught
learn	learned	do	done
notice	noticed	be	been
happen	happened	finish	finished
manage	managed	eat	eaten
cook	cooked	repair	repaired

INFORMATION GAP

HANDOUT 7-B

Chorba is a Romanian stew. Nicolae and Victor's mother made it when they were sick. Below is a recipe for *bigos*, a Polish stew.

 ♦ Work with a partner.
 ♦ Ask and answer questions to find the missing information.
 ♦ Write the information on the blanks. Ask questions like this:

 A: *How much* __flour__ *do I need?* B: ____1____ *cup.*

INGREDIENTS A

____ cup flour	2 pounds sauerkraut, rinsed and drained
1 teaspoon each paprika and caraway seed	____ medium onions, sliced
____ tablespoons butter	12 ounces Polish sausage, cut in 1-inch pieces
1 pound lean beef, cut in cubes	____ pound mushrooms, sliced
____ pound lean pork, cut in cubes	1/2 cup dry white wine

DIRECTIONS: Combine _____, _____, and _____. Coat the pieces of meat with the flour. Heat the _____ in a large pot. Add the meat and brown it. Add the _____, onion, sausage, mushrooms, and wine. Cover and cook over low heat for $1^1/_2$ to 2 hours. Serve with small _____ potatoes.

✂ -

Chorba is a Romanian stew. Nicolae and Victor's mother made it when they were sick. Below is a recipe for *bigos,* a Polish stew.

 ♦ Work with a partner.
 ♦ Ask and answer questions to find the missing information.
 ♦ Write the information on the blanks. Ask questions like this:

 B: *How much* __beef__ *do I need?* A: __1 pound__ .

INGREDIENTS B

1 cup flour	____ pounds sauerkraut, rinsed and drained
____ teaspoon each paprika and caraway seed	2 medium onions, sliced
2 tablespoons butter	____ ounces Polish sausage, cut in 1-inch pieces
____ pound lean beef, cut in cubes	1/2 pound mushrooms, sliced
1 pound lean pork, cut in cubes	____ cup dry white wine

DIRECTIONS: Combine flour, paprika, and caraway seeds. Coat the pieces of _____ with the flour. Heat the butter in a large pot. Add the meat and _____ it. Add the sauerkraut, _____, sausage, mushrooms, and wine. Cover and cook over low heat for _____ hours. Serve with small, boiled potatoes.

Reproducible Handouts ══ **39**

TELL THE STORY

HANDOUT 7-C

Think about Nicolae's dream.

♦ Work with a partner or a small group.
♦ Write one more sentence about Nicolae's dream in the blank box.
♦ Cut cards and scramble them.
♦ Work together to put Nicolae's dream in order.
♦ Take turns telling the dream to another pair or group.

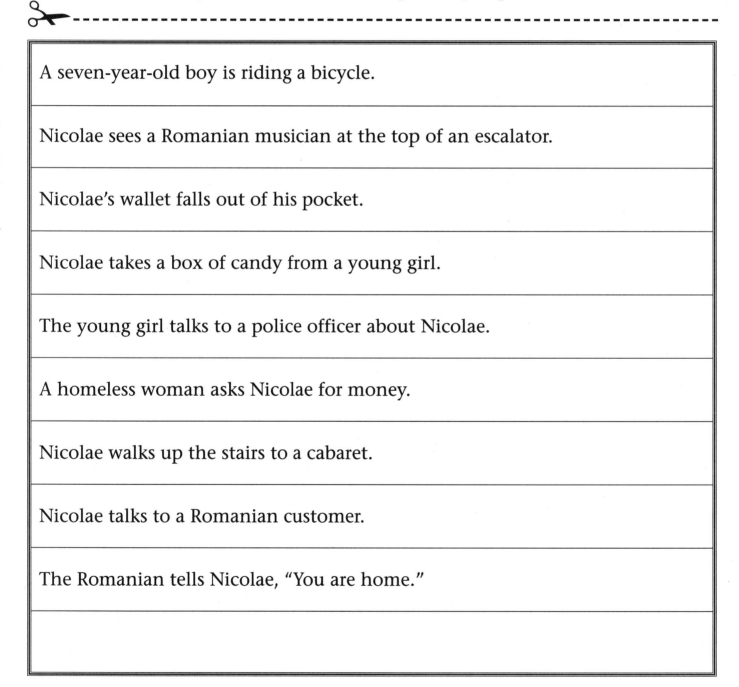

A seven-year-old boy is riding a bicycle.
Nicolae sees a Romanian musician at the top of an escalator.
Nicolae's wallet falls out of his pocket.
Nicolae takes a box of candy from a young girl.
The young girl talks to a police officer about Nicolae.
A homeless woman asks Nicolae for money.
Nicolae walks up the stairs to a cabaret.
Nicolae talks to a Romanian customer.
The Romanian tells Nicolae, "You are home."

INTERVIEW

HANDOUT 7-D

On his first day in the United States, Nicolae met the employees at Crossroads Café and he ate Rosa's soup. Think about your first day in the United States.

- ◆ Interview a partner about his or her first day in the United States.
- ◆ Ask the questions below or make up your own questions.
- ◆ Write your partner's answers on the lines.
- ◆ Share the interview with another pair.

NAME:	INTERVIEWER:
1. When did you come to the United States?	
2. How did you travel to the United States?	
3. Where did you first arrive?	
4. Who was with you?	
5. What do you remember about your first day?	
6. Who met you?	
7. What were you wearing?	
8. What did you eat?	
9. How did you feel?	
10. Did anything unusual happen? If yes, explain.	

Katherine is very tired and worried. Her son, David, doesn't like to do school work. David will have a birthday soon; he will be 14 years old.

Henry is happy and full of energy. He is dating Sara, a girl from school. Sara is in Henry's social studies class.

Everyone at Crossroads Café is worried about Katherine. They want to help her, but she won't talk about her problems.

Katherine asks Jamal about computers. She shows him an ad for a computer in a catalogue. This computer is cheaper than the other computers. Jamal says, "It's a close out." The computer is cheap because it is not a new model.

Katherine comes home from work. Her children are fighting. David wants to watch a football game. Suzanne, David's eight-year-old sister, doesn't. Katherine tells them to take turns choosing TV programs.

David is not happy. He has to babysit his sister after school. He can't be with his friends. He asks his mother, "Why do you have to work this second job anyway?"

Katherine is working two jobs because she wants to buy David a computer for his birthday. It's a surprise. Katherine can't tell David and Suzanne the truth about her second job.

Sara comes to Crossroads Café to see Henry. She tells him about a formal dance at school.

Rosa asks Henry about the school dance. Henry is not going to the dance because he doesn't know how to dance. Rosa offers to teach him. Sara comes into the café and sees Henry dancing with Rosa. Sara is jealous and walks out.

Rosa asks Katherine to go shopping after work. Katherine says no. She has no time. Rosa's feelings are hurt. Later that evening, Rosa goes to Katherine's apartment. Suzanne is alone. She tells Rosa about Katherine's second job.

Suzanne is drawing a picture. Rosa looks at it. Suzanne drew two unhappy children. Then Katherine comes home. She is surprised and a little angry to see Rosa. Rosa shows Suzanne's drawing to Katherine. She feels very sad when she sees the drawing. Then David comes home and argues with his mother.

The next day at work, Katherine is upset. David would not talk to her in the morning. She calls home after school, but the children are not there.

Finally Katherine tells Mr. Brashov and the other employees about her second job. While she is talking to them, the door to the café opens. It is David and Suzanne. David fixed Jess's airplane. He is bringing it to Jess.

Katherine doesn't see David and Suzanne, but they hear her. They do not want money. They want to be with their mother. They love her. Katherine decides to celebrate David's birthday early. She will take her children to the lake for a long weekend.

Then Sara comes to the café to talk to Henry. He explains about Rosa. He says, "I can't dance and Rosa was teaching me." Henry asks Sara to go to the school dance.

     Reproducible Handouts

THINK AND SPEAK

HANDOUT 8-A

Think about things you would like someone to offer to do for you. Then think about things you would offer to do for someone else.

- ♦ Complete the ideas on the cards below.
- ♦ Write your own ideas on the blank cards.
- ♦ Cut out the cards and put them face up in two piles.
- ♦ Work with a partner. Take turns. Use your cards to request help or make offers.

EXAMPLE: A: *Would you like me to help with the laundry?*   B: *Sure.*
          OR
          A: *I'll help you with the laundry.*   B: *Thanks.*

THINGS I WOULD LIKE SOMEONE TO HELP ME WITH . . .	THINGS I WOULD HELP SOMEONE ELSE DO . . .
fold the	take care of
put away the	deliver
scrub the	clean
replace the	cook
paint the	take
hold the	go

INTERVIEW

HANDOUT 8-B

Do you have a computer? Do you use one at work?

- ♦ Talk about computers with a partner or small group.
- ♦ Ask the questions in the chart.
- ♦ Share the answers with the rest of the class.

	NAME:		NAME:		NAME:	
	YES	NO	YES	NO	YES	NO
1. Do you have a computer at home?						
If yes, what kind?						
If no, do you plan to buy one? Why or why not?						
2. Do you use a computer at work?						
3. Do you use a computer at school?						
4. If you have children, do they use computers at school?						
5. What do you like about computers?						
6. What do you dislike about computers?						

GIVE YOUR OPINION

HANDOUT 8-C

People have many different ideas and attitudes about children. What's your opinion about the statements below?

♦ Work with a partner or small group.
♦ Cut and scramble the statement cards, and then put them face down.
♦ One learner turns over a card and reads it aloud.
♦ Learners agree or disagree with the statement and tell why.

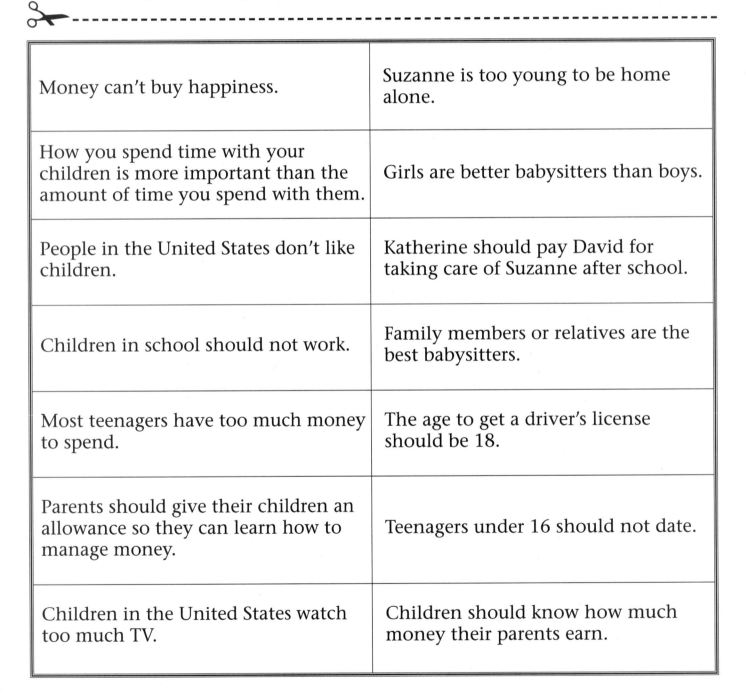

Money can't buy happiness.	Suzanne is too young to be home alone.
How you spend time with your children is more important than the amount of time you spend with them.	Girls are better babysitters than boys.
People in the United States don't like children.	Katherine should pay David for taking care of Suzanne after school.
Children in school should not work.	Family members or relatives are the best babysitters.
Most teenagers have too much money to spend.	The age to get a driver's license should be 18.
Parents should give their children an allowance so they can learn how to manage money.	Teenagers under 16 should not date.
Children in the United States watch too much TV.	Children should know how much money their parents earn.

SOLVE THE PROBLEM

HANDOUT 8-D

Katherine is a single parent. Do you know any single parents? What problems do Katherine and other single parents have?

- ♦ Work with a partner or a small group.
- ♦ Read the problem cards.
- ♦ Write one more problem on the blank card.
- ♦ Choose one or two problems to discuss.
- ♦ Make one or two suggestions to solve the problems.
- ♦ Share the suggestions with the class.

PROBLEM #1 David and Suzanne don't know why their parents are divorced. They blame their mother for the divorce, and they're angry with her.
What should their mother, Katherine, tell them?

PROBLEM #2 Suzanne is eight years old. She is too young to be alone after school. But Suzanne's brother, David, doesn't want to take care of her everyday after school. He wants to play basketball after school. Sometimes David also needs to stay after school to get help from his teachers.
What should Katherine do?

PROBLEM #3 Maria is a single parent. She has been divorced for three years. Her children are 12 and 13 years old. Maria works long hours and gets paid a lot of overtime. Her children are not happy. But Maria needs the overtime money to pay the bills.
What can she do?

PROBLEM #4 Tom is a single parent. His wife died two years ago. Tom has three-year-old twin boys. Tom's family lives in another state. He has no relatives to help him. The twins go to a daycare center. But sometimes Tom has to work late and the daycare center closes at 6:00 P.M.
What can Tom do?

PROBLEM # 5

UNIT 9   RUSH TO JUDGMENT

Two police detectives are in Crossroads Café. Mr. Brashov met them last week. Henry comes into the café with his grandparents. Mr. Brashov introduces Henry to the police officers. Henry's grandparents are afraid of the police. The police were not very nice to them in China. Henry doesn't think the police are very nice in the U.S., but Mr. Brashov disagrees with him.

Henry's grandparents don't speak much English. They are going to take the bus to the senior citizens' center for flu shots. Henry gives them a map and takes them to a bus stop.

Jamal is late for work. He is walking down the street with his toolbox. The toolbox opens and the tools fall out. Two policemen are watching from a car. When they see Jamal's tools, they get out of their car. They ask Jamal for identification. He does not have his wallet or his driver's license.

The police ask Jamal, "Where were you last night around 11:30?" Jamal was home with his wife and sick daughter. The police want to check Jamal's story with his wife. But Jamal's wife is out of town on business. The police do not like Jamal's answers to their questions. They decide to take him to the police station.

Jamal calls Mr. Brashov. Jamal is very upset and Mr. Brashov cannot understand him. Mr. Brashov tells Jess and Katherine, "It's something about burglaries." Jess saw an article in the newspaper about some recent burglaries. The description of the burglar sounds like Jamal.

Mr. Brashov goes to the police station. He waits a long time to see Jamal. Nobody answers Mr. Brashov's questions.

While Jamal and Mr. Brashov are at the police station, Henry comes back to the café. His grandparents are lost. They did not go to the senior citizens' center. Jess offers to help Henry look for his grandparents.

Jess and Henry cannot find the two old people, so they return to the café. Then Henry's mother comes in. She wants to take her parents home. Henry doesn't want to tell his mother the truth. Jess helps Henry. He tells Henry's mother, "I'll drive your parents home when they come back to the café."

At the police station, one of the detectives recognizes Mr. Brashov. Mr. Brashov identifies Jamal, and he gives him an alibi. Mr. Brashov was talking to Jamal on the phone at the time of the robbery. He heard Jamal's crying baby. The police finally let Jamal go.

Mr. Brashov and Jamal go to Crossroads Café. Rosa gives Jamal something to eat, but he is not hungry. He is very angry and sad. Jess asks, "What happened out there, Jamal?" Jamal does not want to tell the story. Katherine tells him to file a complaint. Mr. Brashov tells him to forget about it. Jamal says, "Now I know how it feels to be treated badly because of the way you look."

A police officer enters the café with Henry's grandparents. The police officer found them wandering the streets. He helped them find the café. Jess takes them home.

    Reproducible Handouts   **49**

CATEGORIES

HANDOUT 9-A

Jess read about a burglar in the newspaper. The burglar's description was the same as Jamal's.

- ♦ Work with a partner.
- ♦ Add two or more names to the blank cards.
- ♦ Cut the cards, scramble them, and put them face down in a pile.
- ♦ Take turns. Turn over a card and describe the person to your partner. Your partner takes notes.
- ♦ Choose one person and use your notes to draw him or her.
- ♦ Share your drawing with the class.

- -

Your English teacher	A relative
Your partner	A classmate
A neighbor	A famous person
Your best friend	Your favorite actor

DIALOGUE

HANDOUT 9-B

Henry's grandparents are missing. Rosa, Katherine, and Jess try to help Henry find them.

- ◆ Work with a partner.
- ◆ Read the dialogue cards below.
- ◆ Cut out the cards, scramble them and place them face up on the table.
- ◆ While you watch the video, put the conversation in order.
- ◆ Share with another pair. Is the order of the cards the same?

✂ -

JESS: You didn't lose them. They got lost.
ROSA: Maybe you should call 9-1-1.
KATHERINE: What about the map you use for your deliveries?
JESS: Rosa, can you hand me that bottle of ketchup?
JESS: Don't worry. We can get one at the newsstand.
MRS. CHANG: Henry, where are your grandparents? Your father is parked outside.
HENRY: They just stepped out.
JESS: Mrs. Chang, I'm Jess Washington.
MRS. CHANG: Oh no. That would be a terrible imposition.
ROSA: Henry, what did she say?

ROLE-PLAY

HANDOUT 9-C

Think about Henry's grandparents and Jamal. What could they tell other people about their experiences with the police?

- ◆ Work with a partner or small group.
- ◆ Cut out the cards and turn them face down on the table.
- ◆ Have one person pick a card, read it aloud, and pick a partner to do the role-play.
- ◆ Share one or two of the role-plays with the rest of the class.

✂ -

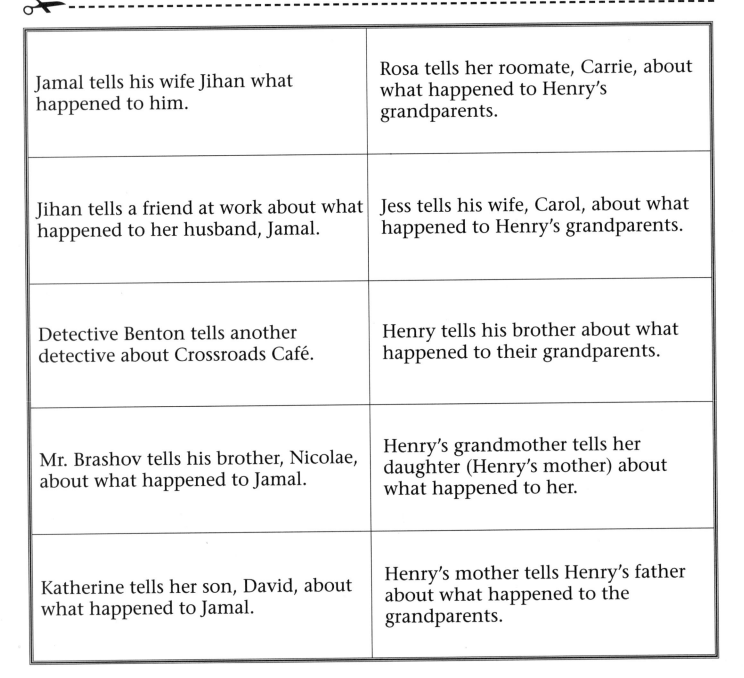

Jamal tells his wife Jihan what happened to him.	Rosa tells her roomate, Carrie, about what happened to Henry's grandparents.
Jihan tells a friend at work about what happened to her husband, Jamal.	Jess tells his wife, Carol, about what happened to Henry's grandparents.
Detective Benton tells another detective about Crossroads Café.	Henry tells his brother about what happened to their grandparents.
Mr. Brashov tells his brother, Nicolae, about what happened to Jamal.	Henry's grandmother tells her daughter (Henry's mother) about what happened to her.
Katherine tells her son, David, about what happened to Jamal.	Henry's mother tells Henry's father about what happened to the grandparents.

INTERVIEW

HANDOUT 9-D

Jamal had a bad experience with the police. Henry's grandparents had a good experience. Think about your experiences with police.

- ♦ Interview a partner about the police.
- ♦ Write your partner's answers on the lines below.
- ♦ Share your interview with the rest of the class.

NAME:	INTERVIEWER:
1. Have you ever been stopped by the police in the United States?	
2. What happened?	
3. How did you feel?	
4. Did you understand the police when they talked to you?	
5. How did the police treat you? Were they polite or rude? Give examples.	
6. Have you ever been stopped by the police in another country?	
7. What happened?	
8. How did you feel?	
9. Compare the police in the United States to the police in your country. How are they the same or different?	
10. Would Jamal's experience be the same in your native country?	

UNIT 10 — LET THE BUYER BEWARE

It's Monday morning. Mr. Brashov is doing paperwork at his desk. Business is not good at Crossroads Café. There are not enough customers. Mr. Brashov is worried.

Later in the afternoon, the café is almost empty. One customer is sitting at the counter. Jess and Mr. Brashov are watching the customer. He asks Katherine for coffee. Then he asks for water. Finally he asks Katherine for her name. He introduces himself. His name is Bill. Katherine isn't very interested in Bill.

An attractive woman comes into the café. She wants to order some dessert. Katherine suggests lemon meringue pie or Mr. Brashov's special apple strudel. The woman orders the apple strudel and she loves it. Mr. Brashov introduces himself to the woman. Her name is Barbara. She is very friendly to Mr. Brashov. Before Barbara leaves the café, she invites Mr. Brashov to have dinner with her.

Mr. Brashov and Barbara go to Palmettos, an expensive restaurant. Barbara tells Mr. Brashov, "I'm a friend of the owner. I helped him win an important award." Barbara helps restaurant owners find customers. She wants to help Mr. Brashov.

Mr. Brashov likes Barbara a lot. They see a lot of each other. Mr. Brashov gives Barbara money to find more customers for Crossroads Café. But Rosa doesn't trust Barbara. She has a bad feeling about her.

Bill asks Katherine to go out for dinner. She says no because she doesn't have a babysitter. Rosa offers to babysit, and Katherine agrees to meet Bill at Palmettos.

The excellent service surprises Katherine. Bill tells her, "My father owns Palmettos." Then Katherine sees Barbara. She is supposed to be out of town, but she is eating dinner with a man. He gives money to Barbara. Katherine gets up quickly and calls Rosa. Katherine tells Bill the problem. Bill thinks of a plan and asks his father for help.

Jamal appears at Palmettos. He has a moustache, and he is dressed like a waiter. He brings a dessert tray to Barbara and her date. Jamal uses a very small camera to take a picture of Barbara and her date.

When the pictures are developed, Katherine shows them to Mr. Brashov. His feelings are hurt and he is angry. He liked Barbara. He also gave her $800 to advertise Crossroads Café.

Mr. Brashov has a plan to get his money back from Barbara. Bill's father, the owner of Palmettos, helps him. First, Mr. Brashov puts an ad in the newspaper for half price lunch specials. Next, he borrows Palmettos's award from Bill's father.

When Barbara comes to the café she is surprised to see so many people. She watches two men in suits give money to Mr. Brashov. Barbara asks Mr. Brashov about them. They are investors, he tells Barbara. He also tells Barbara he won an award.

Barbara wants to invest in the Crossroads's Café, too. Mr. Brashov asks for $900, but he agrees to accept $800.00. After Barbara gives Mr. Brashov the money, he tells her to get out of the café. Barbara screams and yells. Everyone claps when she leaves.

Katherine thanks Bill for his help. Then he asks her for another date. She accepts, on one condition. No restaurants.

THINK AND SPEAK

HANDOUT 10-A

Practice giving compliments.

- ◆ Work with a partner or small group.
- ◆ Copy topics for compliments on the blank cards.
- ◆ Cut and scramble the cards and place them face down in a pile.
- ◆ Take turns: one person picks a card, reads it, and gives a compliment. Use one or more of the expressions below.
- ◆ Another person responds to the compliment.

EXAMPLE: *You are* _____.

Your _____ *is* _____.

You are a very _____ _____.

Your _____ *is a* _____.

✂ -

DIALOGUE

HANDOUT 10-B

Mr. Brashov and Barbara are having dinner at Palmettos. What are they saying to each other?

- ◆ Work with a partner and read the cards.
- ◆ Cut, scramble, and place them face up on the table.
- ◆ While you watch the video, put the cards in order.
- ◆ Share with another pair. Is the order of the cards the same?

- -

MR. BRASHOV: Please take the last bite.
MR. BRASHOV: Well, if you insist.
MR. BRASHOV: The food is magnificent.
MR. BRASHOV: What is a promoter?
BARBARA: I'm good friends with the owner of Palmettos.
BARBARA: And Victor, I can help you win an award, too.
BARBARA: Victor, you're a smart man.
BARBARA: Victor, please. Tonight you're my guest.
BARBARA: Oh, by the way, I have tickets for a concert tomorrow night.
MR. BRASHOV: It would be my pleasure.

INTERVIEW

HANDOUT 10-C

On their first date, Katherine and Bill went out to dinner. Think about first dates.

- ◆ Interview someone about his or her first date.
- ◆ Ask the questions below or make up your own.
- ◆ Write the answers to the questions on the lines.
- ◆ Ask for permission to share the interview with the rest of the class.

NAME:	INTERVIEWER:
1. When was your first date?	
2. How old were you?	
3. Who was the person?	
4. Where did you go?	
5. How did you feel?	
6. How did your parents feel?	
7. Where did you meet your date?	
8. Do you still know your first date?	
9. If you don't know this person anymore, would you like to?	
10. Are there any things you would change about your first date? What?	

ROLE-PLAY

HANDOUT 10-D

Read these tips for talking to telephone salespeople with a partner.

WATCH OUT FOR TELEPHONE SCAMS!

Read these tips before you buy anything over the phone.
1. Salespeople must tell you their company's name and what they are selling.
2. It's illegal to call before 8:00 A.M. or after 9:00 P.M.
3. Telemarketers can't call you repeatedly or threaten you.
4. Companies must take you off their lists if you ask them to do so.
5. If you win a contest, it's illegal to ask you to pay for the prize.
6. Companies must tell you if there are no refunds.
7. Never give your bank account number to anyone.
8. You can't be required to pay shipping charges for prizes you win in a contest.

- Work with a partner or a small group.
- Cut and scramble the cards. Put them face down in a pile.
- Take turns. Pick a card. Role-play the situation with a partner.
- Share a role-play with the rest of the class.

✂ -

A salesperson calls you at 9:30 P.M.	You won a free TV, but the sales person wants you to pay shipping costs to receive it.
You just won a cruise, but you have to pay a $500 fee.	You won a diamond watch. The telephone salesperson wants your bank account number because you have to pay taxes.
You hang up on a salesperson. The salesperson calls you names and calls again every five minutes for two hours.	You asked this salesperson to stop calling you. He didn't.
You bought a CD over the phone. You changed your mind and you don't want it.	The salesperson will not tell you the name of the company he/she works for.

UNIT 11 NO VACANCY

It's early in the morning. Mr. Brashov is alone in the café, and he hears a noise. He's worried, but it's Henry. Henry is on his way to school, but he forgot something in his locker. Henry takes everything out of the locker. Finally he finds it—a "how-to" video. It gives instructions about how to operate a video camera. Henry has to make a video for his journalism class at school.

Rosa is tired. She isn't sleeping well because of the water pipes in her apartment. They make a lot of noise. Katherine says, "Maybe you should move."

Rosa saw a "for rent" sign on Katherine's building. She decides to look at the apartment after work. She calls for an appointment. The apartment manager is Katherine's friend.

Rosa meets with Dorothy Walsh, the apartment manager, after work. Rosa loves the apartment. She fills out an application form and gives it to Dorothy. Rosa uses Katherine's name for a reference. Dorothy says, "I'll call you."

Rosa waits for Dorothy to call. She is very anxious and excited about the apartment. Then, Dorothy calls Crossroads Café. Rosa is very happy to hear from her. But Dorothy doesn't give Rosa good news. Dorothy is sorry. She says, "The apartment is rented." Rosa is very disappointed.

Rosa tells everyone about Dorothy's call. Jess doesn't believe Dorothy. He says, "It sounds like discrimination to me." Dorothy is Katherine's friend, so she doesn't agree with Jess.

After work, Katherine talks to Dorothy. Dorothy is showing the apartment to Don Peterson and his daughter, Patty. Katherine is shocked and angry with Dorothy. Dorothy says unkind words about Rosa because she is Mexican.

At work the next day, Katherine tells everyone about Dorothy. Rosa wants to forget about it. But Jess, Jamal, and Henry say no. There are laws against discrimination, but it is hard to prove.

Henry has a plan, and everyone agrees to help him. On Saturday, Henry hides in the empty apartment with his video camera. Then Dorothy comes into the apartment with Don and Patty. She tells them, "You'll be comfortable here. I don't rent to undesirable people."

Suddenly, Mr. Brashov and Jess come into the apartment. Jess wants to rent the apartment. Then Jamal comes in. He wants to rent the apartment, too. Dorothy tells them to leave. She doesn't want their type of people in the building.

Henry comes into view with his camera. He videotaped everything. Now Rosa can prove discrimination. Katherine and Rosa enter the apartment. Dorothy is furious. Katherine tells her, "You and I are no longer friends." Don and Patty decide to look for another apartment.

Dorothy offers the apartment to Rosa. But Rosa doesn't want it anymore. She says, "I don't like the view."

Rosa is going to file a complaint against Dorothy. Katherine will be her witness. And Henry has the proof of discrimination on tape. He will also use the tape for his video project. Henry will call it, *Discrimination in Housing: A Case Study.*

FOLLOW THE DIRECTIONS

HANDOUT 11-A

Jamal helped Henry learn to use the video camera. When Henry didn't understand, he asked Jamal questions.

- ◆ Work with a partner or a small group.
- ◆ Two cards are blank. Write or draw your own ideas on them.
- ◆ Cut and scramble the cards and put them face down in a pile.
- ◆ Take turns: one person turns over a card and tells the other person what to do or draw.
- ◆ The other person follows the directions.
- ◆ If you don't understand, say: *Can you say that again? What does that mean? What do you mean? I don't understand. Can you repeat that?*

✂ -

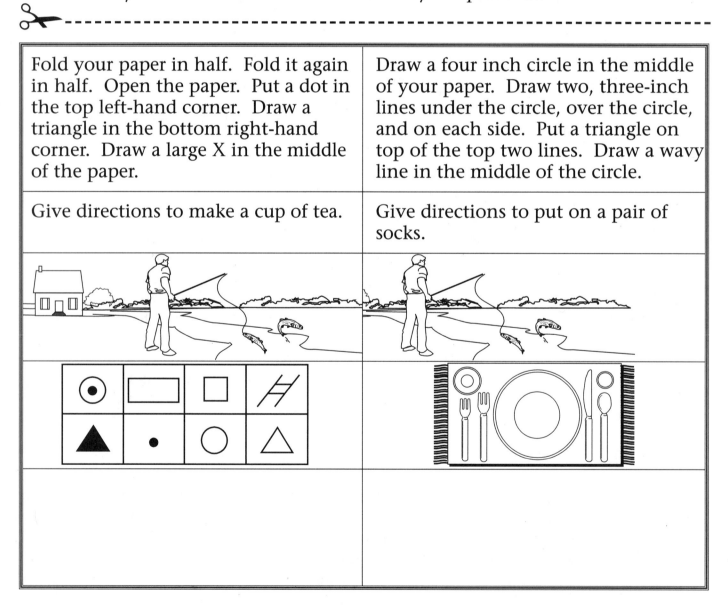

Fold your paper in half. Fold it again in half. Open the paper. Put a dot in the top left-hand corner. Draw a triangle in the bottom right-hand corner. Draw a large X in the middle of the paper.	Draw a four inch circle in the middle of your paper. Draw two, three-inch lines under the circle, over the circle, and on each side. Put a triangle on top of the top two lines. Draw a wavy line in the middle of the circle.
Give directions to make a cup of tea.	Give directions to put on a pair of socks.

HANDOUT 11-B

The words on the cards come from the video and the worktext. Put them in categories.

♦ Work with a partner.
♦ Cut the cards on the lines and put them face up in a pile.
♦ Organize the words into categories.
♦ Write the categories on a piece of paper and put the words under them.
♦ Share your categories with another pair of learners. Are they the same or different?

✂ -

apartment	videotape	reference
application	right	evict
discrimination	wrong	prejudice
lease	tape measure	revenge
manager	video cassette	undesirable
rent	complaint	patient
rental	accent	rented
video camera	focus control	property

SCRAMBLED SENTENCES

HANDOUT 11-C

Dorothy Walsh discriminated against Rosa. The scrambled sentences below tell what happened. Cut out the words.

- ◆ Work with a partner.
- ◆ Put the words of the scrambled sentences in the correct order.
- ◆ Read the sentences. Add capital letters and periods.
- ◆ Add one more sentence about what happened.
- ◆ Write your sentence on the blank cards.
- ◆ Share your sentences with the rest of the class.

✂ --

looked	Katherine's	at	in
apartment	Rosa	building	an

a	filled	rental	form
out	application	she	

like	Mexicans	not	did
property	the	manager	

already	was	Rosa	apartment
she	the	told	rented

made	discrimination	Henry	a
to	videotape	prove	

rent	the	apartment	Rosa
Dorothy	to	to	offered

complaint	file	to	appointment
Rosa	an	a	made

Rosa's	witnesses	and	agreed
Katherine	Henry	be	to

SOLVE THE PROBLEM

HANDOUT 11-D

Dorothy Walsh does not want to rent apartments to undesirables—people like Rosa, Jess, and Jamal. She discriminates against them.

♦ Work with a partner or small group.
♦ Read the problems below.
♦ Decide what to do about each problem.
♦ Write one more problem. Give it to another pair or group to solve.
♦ Choose one problem to role-play for the rest of the class.

PROBLEM #1   You and a group of classmates decide to go out for coffee after class. Two people are from Vietnam, one person is from Mexico, one person is from Nigeria, and another is from Syria. You see several empty tables, but the waitress tells you there are no tables.

PROBLEM #2   You and your spouse want to buy a house. You have saved enough money for a 20% down payment. You both have good jobs and you have no debts. You choose a house in a nice neighborhood. You pay $300 to apply for a mortgage. Then the bank calls. The loan officer says you don't make enough money to buy a house.

PROBLEM #3   You want a better job. You see a notice for an interesting job in another department at your company. You have all of the qualifications. You apply for the job, but you don't get it. Another person without the qualifications gets the job.

PROBLEM #4   You are salesperson in a department store. A customer wants to return something. The customer does not have a receipt. You tell the customer you cannot give her a refund. She refuses to believe you. She says you won't give her money because she doesn't speak English well.

PROBLEM #5

UNIT 12 TURNING POINTS

Mr. Brashov has the key to Crossroads Café in his hand. But the door is already open and there is broken glass on the ground. When he walks into the café, he is shocked. Everything is a mess. The tables and chairs are on the floor. There are broken glasses, bottles, and dishes. There is graffiti on the walls.

Rosa enters the café. At first she doesn't see the mess. Then she tells Mr. Brashov to call the police. Mr. Brashov and Rosa go to the back room. There is more vandalism there. And Mr. Brashov finds a knife with Chinese writing. It is in the wall. Rosa says, "This is the work of a gang."

Mr. Brashov takes the knife from the wall. He thinks the knife belongs to Henry. He will return it to him. Rosa thinks the knife is a message from the gang.

Katherine and Jamal come to work. They are very sad and upset. Mr. Brashov cannot open the café for business. Everyone will work hard to clean the café.

Police Detective Rizzo comes to the café. He agrees with Rosa about the gang. After the detective leaves, Rosa gives the knife to Henry. He is surprised to see it.

Henry is at home. His younger brother Edward and his mother are arguing about Edward's schoolwork. He is not turning in his work on time. Edward complains about his mother to Henry. Edward is very angry with her.

Edward throws darts at a dartboard. Henry throws the knife with Chinese writing at the dartboard. Edward says, "Hey, where did you get that?" Henry doesn't say anything. He just takes the knife and leaves.

Crossroads Café is closed. Katherine and Mr. Brashov are working. The door opens. It's Rosa. She's late to work because the bus was late. Katherine has good news for Rosa. Her neighbor has a used car for sale. If Rosa buys the car, she won't have to take the bus.

Rosa is not excited by Katherine's news. She is embarrassed. Rosa doesn't know how to drive. She has a learner's permit, but she has no time to practice. Jamal and Jess offer to help Rosa.

Henry is talking to Edward at home. Henry asks Edward about the knife. Edward doesn't want to talk. He tries to push Henry out of the way, but Henry throws him to the floor. Edward's shirt rips. Henry sees bruises all over Edward. Finally, Edward talks.

Edward is having problems with a gang. They want him to join. When he tries to avoid them, they beat him. Edward had to give money to the gang. He had to steal from the principal at his school. He had to break into Crossroads Café.

A few days later, a police officer comes into Crossroads Café with Edward. The police officer says, "We think this punk broke into your restaurant. His brother works here." Everyone is shocked. Then the police officer shows Edward's knife to Mr. Brashov. Henry has to tell Mr. Brashov about his brother and the gang.

Mr. Brashov has an idea. Edward and the gang break into Crossroads Café again. But this time, Mr. Brashov is there. And so are all the café employees, people from the neighborhood, and the police. When the police take away the gang, everyone cheers.

ROLE-PLAY

HANDOUT 12-A

The gang members might beat Edward for helping the police. Or they might leave him alone. When you don't know what will happen, use **might**.

- Work with a partner or a small group.
- Each person writes another situation on the blank cards.
- Cut and scramble the cards then put them face down in a pile.
- Take turns. One person turns over a card and reads it.
- The other person(s) tell what **might** happen.
- Each pair or group shares one situation with the rest of the class.

✂ -

You get on the bus to go to work. You don't have any change.	You find a wallet on the street and you return it to the owner.
You buy an instant lottery ticket.	You apply for a new job.
You are on the highway and you run out of gas.	You go to a new restaurant.
You decide to get a haircut.	You change English classes.
You get a phone call from an old friend.	You decide to learn how to play the piano.
You ask your boss for a raise.	You have a car accident.
You enter a contest.	You have an argument with your boss.

CATEGORIES

HANDOUT 12-B

Many communities in the United States have problems with gangs. Gangs often communicate with graffiti. The words and symbols have special meanings. Do you recognize gang graffiti?

- ◆ Work with a partner or small group.
- ◆ Put the cards in a pile.
- ◆ Take turns. Pick up one card at a time.
- ◆ Discuss the picture. Do gangs use this in their graffiti? Decide YES or NO.
- ◆ Put the YES pictures in one pile and the NO pictures in another.
- ◆ Share with the class.

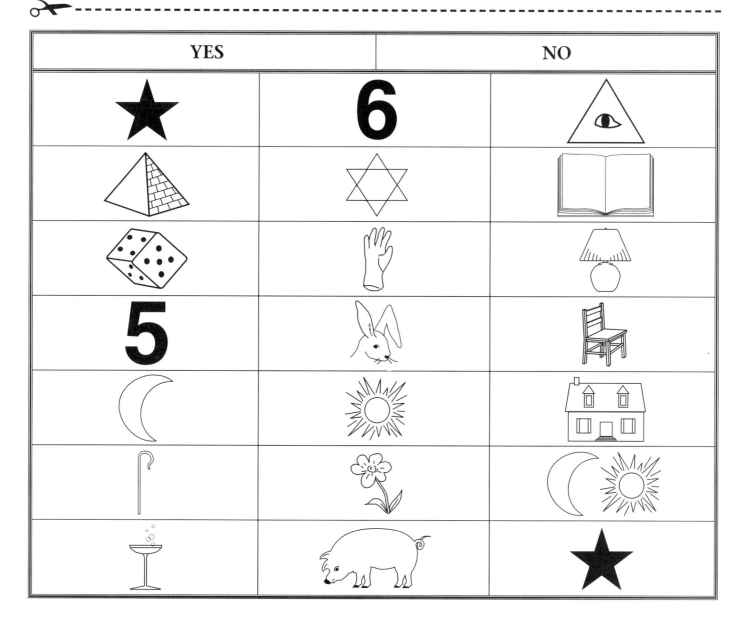

YES		NO

INTERVIEW

HANDOUT 12-C

Mr. Brashov had a plan to help Edward. When the gang came to Crossroads Café the second time, Mr. Brashov, his neighbors, and the police were waiting. What do you think might happen?

♦ Answer the questions.
♦ Interview a partner. Write your partner's answers in the chart.
♦ Share your chart with another pair or group.

	I THINK		YOU THINK	
THINK ABOUT CROSSROADS CAFE	YES	NO	YES	NO
1. Will the gang go to jail?				
2. Will the gang beat Edward again?				
3. Will Mr. Brashov have more trouble with the gang?				
4. Will Edward have problems at school with the gang?				
5. Will Mr. and Mrs. Chang move to get Edward away from the gang?				
6. Will the gang bother other people in the neighborhood?				
7. Will the police help the community fight the gangs?				
THINK ABOUT WHERE YOU LIVE				
8. Are there gangs in your neighborhood or community?				
9. Do you see a lot of gang graffiti?				
10. Are you afraid of gangs?				

VOCABULARY BINGO

HANDOUT 12-D

B	I	N	G	O
GRAFFITI	KNIFE	BEAT UP	JOIN	PROPERTY
BRUISES	VANDALIZED	BREAK IN	INVESTIGATION	CATCH
SPRAY PAINT	POLICE	**FREE SPACE**	CRIME	SURROUND
GANG	HANDCUFFS	SUSPECTS	DESTROYED	INSTALL
FINGERPRINTS	SECURITY	EVIDENCE	OVERTURNED	SHATTERED

Reproducible Handouts

Mr. Brashov is at Crossroads Café. Rosa brings him fish to eat. He is not happy. Mr. Brashov wanted a hamburger and french fries. Rosa wants Mr. Brashov to eat fish. It is better for his health.

Mr. Brashov talks about his dream vacation. First he will drive to Niagara Falls. Then he will camp and fish. But Mr. Brashov cannot take a vacation. He has too much to do at Crossroads Café. If he goes on a vacation, who will manage the café? Jess tells Mr. Brashov to take his dream vacation with his daughter. But Mr. Brashov and his daughter do not get along with each other.

Jess and his wife, Carol, have problems, too. Carol has a job and Jess does not. He is retired. Carol buys Jess a watch, but he is not happy. He thinks it costs too much. They argue about the watch. Carol says she'll return it.

That night, Mr. Brashov thinks about Crossroads Café. He has an idea. The employees should learn each other's jobs. The next day at the café, Mr. Brashov talks about his idea. He wants everyone to change jobs for a day. Today they will watch each other. Tomorrow they will trade places. Rosa will manage the café. Katherine will cook. Henry will wait on the customers. Jamal will deliver the food and bus tables. And Mr. Brashov will be the handyman!

Carol wants to go out to a new restaurant for dinner. Jess says no. It's not Saturday. They can't afford to eat out more than once a week. He will cook dinner. Carol is very unhappy. She thinks Jess has problems because he is not working.

Jess goes to Crossroads Café. It is not open, but Mr. Brashov is still there. He is working late on paperwork. Jess and Mr. Brashov talk about their problems.

The next day everyone trades jobs at the café. At first there are no problems. But at lunchtime, there are a lot of customers and a lot of problems. Mr. Brashov and Jess play chess and watch the employees. Katherine doesn't cook fast enough. Jamal doesn't make a food delivery because he can't find the house. Rosa gives some customers the wrong change. Henry drops some food on the floor.

Carol comes into the café to see Jess. She wants to talk to him about their problems. Carol and Jess argue because of the changes in their lives. They have new roles. They are trading places, too.

Mr. Brashov continues to watch everyone in the café. He is laughing. Then he holds his chest and falls to the ground. Katherine calls 911. Mr. Brashov had a heart attack.

CONVERSATION SQUARES

HANDOUT 13-A

Work with a partner. One person is **A** and the other is **B**. Work together to complete the grid below.

- In the *top left-hand box*, write **four** things you both can do well.
- In the *top right-hand box*, write **four** things **A** can do, but **B** can't.
- In the *bottom left-hand box* write **four** things **B** can do, but **A** can't.
- In the *bottom right-hand box* write **four** things neither of you can do well.

BOTH A AND B   **ONLY A**

| | |
| | |

ONLY B   **NEITHER A NOR B**

THINK AND SHARE

HANDOUT 13-B

People who live together have many responsibilities.

♦ Put a check (✔) in the box next to the responsibilities you have.
♦ Check the boxes for other people in your home.
♦ Add two more responsibilities to the list.
♦ Circle the responsibilities you like.
♦ Share your list with a small group. Are your lists the same or different? Why?

RESPONSIBILITY	YOU	MOTHER	FATHER	SISTER	BROTHER	OTHER
cook						
fix the car						
shop for food						
vacuum/sweep the floors						
wash clothes						
talk to children's teachers						
do yardwork						
pay the bills						
iron clothes						
take children to school or pick them up						
do dishes						

MIX AND MATCH

HANDOUT 13-C

♦ Cut the cards and place them in two piles: jobs and responsibilities.

♦ Scramble each pile: half of the learners take job cards and the other half take responsibility cards.

♦ Walk around the room and ask questions to match the jobs and responsibilities.

EXAMPLE: Q: *What do you do?* A: *I _____.*
Q: *Do you _____? Yes, I do.*
No, I don't.

♦ When you find a match, sit down.

✂ -

bus person	cleans tables
waitress	brings food to customers
chef/cook	prepares food
manager	tells everyone what to do
paramedic	gives first aid
customer	eats in a restaurant
handyman	fixes things
delivery person	brings products to people
cashier	takes money from people
actor	pretends to be a different person
professor	teaches
homemaker	takes care of house

DISCUSSION

HANDOUT 13-D

Look at the jobs in the chart below. In your country, who usually performs these jobs? Who usually performs these jobs in the United States? Are your answers for the two countries the same or different?

- ♦ Check the box for your country.
- ♦ Check the box for the United States.
- ♦ Share your answers with a partner or a small group.

JOB	IN MY COUNTRY		IN THE UNITED STATES	
	MEN	WOMEN	MEN	WOMEN
Elementary School Teacher				
Housekeeper				
Doctor				
Lawyer				
Secretary				
Nurse				
Police Officer				
Mechanic				
Engineer				
Librarian				

UNIT **14**   LIFE GOES ON

Mr. Brashov had a heart attack. Rosa went to the hospital with him. Now the employees are waiting to hear from Rosa. They are all very nervous and worried.

Finally Rosa calls. Mr. Brashov had a mild heart attack, but now he is out of danger. Everyone wants to visit him at the hospital. But Mr. Brashov cannot have visitors until the next day.

At the hospital, Mr. Brashov is feeling better. He wants to go back to work. Rosa comes to visit. The nurse says, "Mr. Brashov can't have any visitors until tomorrow. The rules are very strict here." But the nurse lets Rosa stay for a few minutes.

Mr. Brashov introduces Rosa to his roommate, Joe Jenkins. Joe Jenkins has heart problems, too. Mr. Jenkins tells Mr. Brashov, "You are a very lucky man. You are in the hospital, but you are alive."

Mr. Brashov argues with his nurse, Brenda. Then Rosa and Mr. Brashov talk about the café. Mr. Brashov is worried, and he wants to close it. Rosa tells Mr. Brashov to take care of himself. The employees will take care of Crossroads Café.

The next day, Rosa opens the café. Soon the other employees come. Rosa tells them what to do. As always, Rosa and Katherine start to argue. Neither of them can work if the other is the boss. Henry is too young to be the boss. Jamal has to take care of his baby, so he cannot be the boss. Then Jess comes. The employees decide he should be the boss. Jess agrees to manage the café until Mr. Brashov returns.

In the hospital, Mr. Brashov complains a lot. Katherine and Henry come to visit. They tell Mr. Brashov about Jess. Jess is a good manager. He has many ideas about how to improve things at the restaurant. But Mr. Brashov is not happy to hear about Jess's ideas. He is worried. Maybe nobody needs him. Everything is fine at the café without him.

When Jamal visits Mr. Brashov, he also talks about Jess. Mr. Brashov is not happy. Jamal brings Mr. Brashov some food from the café. Brenda will not let him eat it. After Jamal leaves, Mr. Brashov is very depressed.

A young woman comes to Crossroads Café. She wants to speak to Jess. Her name is Anna, and she is Mr. Brashov's daughter. She doesn't visit her father in the hospital. She gives Jess a package for him. Then she leaves.

At the hospital, Mr. Brashov continues to feel better, but his roommate, Mr. Jenkins, dies. Mr. Brashov did not know Mr. Jenkins was so sick. He never complained. Mr. Brashov feels very bad because he complains all of the time.

Several days pass. It is late afternoon, and the café is busy. Then the electricity goes out. Nobody knows what to do. Suddenly, they hear Mr. Brashov's voice. He is out of the hospital.

Jess gives Mr. Brashov the package from his daughter, Anna. When Mr. Brashov opens it, he sees a picture of a little girl. It's his granddaughter. Anna never told him about her. Mr. Brashov is very surprised and happy.

HANDOUT 14-A

Directions: Make sentences with these words.

talk	pneumonia	my
delicious	my	to	goodnight
tired	say	hospital
salty	getting	friend	losing
very	$10.00	strict	are
hot	angry	and	speak	sick
friends	watch	today	read
speak	tasteless	the	working	happy
I'm	TV	going	home
a	work	my	I
sad	worried	cold	too	country
overtime	food	expensive	ticket	visit

ASK AND ANSWER

HANDOUT 14-B

Use descriptive words to talk about how you feel in different situations.

♦ Work with a partner or in a small group.
♦ Take turns asking each other the following questions.
♦ Add two more questions on the lines below.
♦ To respond, each person points to a face and then answers using one of the sentences below.

> EXAMPLE: Q: *How do you feel <u>when you work overtime?</u>*
> A: *I feel <u>tired.</u>*
> *I feel <u>very tired.</u>*
> *I feel <u>too tired to walk!</u>*

Ask Your Partner: "How do you feel when you . . .
♦ work overtime?"
♦ lose $20.00?"
♦ get a speeding ticket?"
♦ have a cold?"
♦ argue with a friend?"
♦ visit your native country?"
♦ visit a friend in the hospital?"
♦ lose your keys?"
♦ buy new clothes?"
♦ get a raise?"
♦ _____
♦ _____

Your partner points to the appropriate face and answers the question.

terrific   good   so so

not so good   terrible   angry

INFORMATION GAP

HANDOUT 14-C

PARTNER A

Directions: Look at this chart of health-care benefits. Ask your partner questions to complete the chart.

> EXAMPLE: Q: *How much do I pay for doctor visits?*
> A: *Nothing. There is no charge.*

BENEFIT	COST	BENEFIT	COST
Doctor Visits		Generic Prescription Drugs	$3 each
Outpatient Psychiatric Care	$20 per visit	Non-Generic Prescription Drugs	
Hospital Services		Birth Control Pills	$8 each
In-Area Emergency	$10 per visit	Mail Order Prescription Drugs	
Emergency Ambulance Transportation		Outpatient Substance Abuse Treatment	$20 per visit
Out-of Area Emergency	$0	Nicotine Patches	

✂ -

PARTNER B

Directions: Look at this chart of health-care benefits. Ask your partner questions to fill in the chart.

> EXAMPLE: Q: *How much do I pay for generic prescription drugs?*
> A: *$3.00 for each.*

BENEFIT	COST	BENEFIT	COST
Doctor Visits	$0	Generic Prescription Drugs	
Outpatient Psychiatric Care		Non-generic Prescription Drugs	$8
Hospital Services	None	Birth Control Pills	
In-Area Emergency		Mail-Order Prescription Drugs	$3
Emergency Ambulance Transportation	None	Outpatient Substance Abuse Treatment	$20 per visit
Out-of-Area Emergency	$0	Nicotine Patches	

CULTURE COMPARISON

HANDOUT 14-D

Think about hospitals in the United States and in your native country.

- ♦ Answer the questions below.
- ♦ Write your answers in the chart.
- ♦ Talk to a partner. Are your answers the same or different?
- ♦ Share your answers with a small group or the rest of the class.

	IN THE UNITED STATES	IN _____
Is it expensive to go to a hospital?		
Do most people have health insurance?		
Does health insurance pay for all medical care costs?		
Do people know their doctors well?		
Do doctors talk to the family about the sick person?		
Can patients have visitors? How many at a time? How often?		
Can children visit patients?		
Do people bring things to patients when they visit? What?		
Can visitors bring food to patients?		

UNIT 15 BREAKING AWAY

There are workmen in the vacant building next to Crossroads Café. Mr. Brashov is happy about the new business because vacant buildings are bad for business.

Sara, Henry's girlfriend, comes in the café. Sara says to Henry, "Did you tell them, yet?" Henry finally says, "Sara and I are going together." But nobody is surprised. They already knew.

Sara wants to tell her parents and Henry's parents that they are going together. Henry doesn't think that's necessary. Sara disagrees. She invites Henry to have dinner at her house on Thursday with her parents.

Henry is eating dinner with his parents. His mother has some news. Old friends, the Fongs, are moving back to town. Their daughter, Karen, is the same age as Henry. Karen and Henry played together when they were young. The Fongs are coming for dinner on Thursday night.

Henry says, "I'm having dinner at Sara's on Thursday." Henry's mother tells him to prepare for disappointment. Sara's parents will be unhappy because Henry is Chinese. Henry disagrees with his mother.

Jamal has news for Mr. Brashov. The new business next door is a laundromat. Mr. Brashov doesn't like this news. He thinks a laundromat will be bad for business. People will come to Crossroads Café for change for the laundry machines, not for food.

Rosa suddenly says, "No water!" At the same time, a woman comes in and asks for change for the pay phone. Her name is Linda, and she is the owner of the laundromat. Linda wants to call the Water and Power Company. Her workmen cannot turn off the water to install the washing machines. Mr. Brashov tells her, "Your workmen turned off my water."

It's Thursday night. Henry is having dinner at the Graysons. First, Mr. Grayson talks about football. Henry hates the Graysons' favorite team. Then Henry talks about hockey. The Graysons are not hockey fans. Next, the Graysons talk about food. This is not a good topic either. Finally Henry says, "Sara and I are going together." This is definitely a bad topic.

Sara's mother asks Henry and Sara to wait for a while. Henry thinks Sara's parents don't approve of him. He gets up from the table and leaves the Grayson home.

There are problems at Crossroads Café, too. Mr. Brashov is angry about his new neighbor again. Now her workmen are repainting the lines in the parking lot.

Henry is very sad. He tells Jamal about his dinner at the Graysons and his problems with Sara. Rosa overhears the discussion. Rosa and Katherine give Henry advice. Henry decides to invite his parents, Sara, and her parents to Crossroads Café to talk.

The Changs and the Graysons are at Crossroads Café. Henry apologizes to the Graysons for his rude behavior. Mr. and Mrs. Grayson explain their feelings about Henry and Sara. They talk about their plans for their daughter's future. After a lot of discussion, all of the parents agree to trust their children.

Mr. Brashov decides he likes his new neighbor after all. Linda's workmen made six new parking places—three for him and three for her.

SAME OR DIFFERENT

HANDOUT 15-A

Work with a partner. One person is **A** and the other is **B**. Work together to complete the grid below.

- In the *top left-hand box*, write **three** things you both like and **three** things you both like to do.
- In the *top right-hand box*, write **three** things A likes but **B** doesn't and **three** things A likes to do but **B** doesn't.
- In the bottom *left-hand box*, write **three** things B likes but A doesn't and **three** things B likes to do but A doesn't.
- In the bottom *right-hand box*, write **three** things neither of you like and **three** things neither of you like to do.

BOTH A AND B	ONLY A
Like	Likes
Like to do	Likes to do
Likes	Like
Likes to do	Like to do

ONLY B	NEITHER A NOR B

INTERVIEW

HANDOUT 15-B

There is a new business next to Crossroads Café. What businesses are in your communities? Which ones do you go to?

- Interview a partner about businesses in his or her community.
- Ask the questions below.
- Write the answers in the chart.
- Talk about the questions below the chart with your partner.
- Share your answers with another pair.

NAME:	INTERVIEWER:		
What businesses do you go to in your community?	What are the names of the businesses?	Why do you go there?	How often do you go there?
1.			
2.			
3.			
4.			
5.			
6.			

Do you go to any of these businesses? _____

Which ones? _____

Which businesses do you like? Why? Why do you think they are successful?

_____

_____

CATEGORIES

HANDOUT 15-C

FACT: Crossroads Café is a restaurant. INFERENCE: Crossroads Café is busy because the food is good. What's the difference between a fact and an inference?

- ♦ Work with a partner or a small group.
- ♦ Write two more FACTS and INFERENCES on the blank cards.
- ♦ Cut the cards on the lines.
- ♦ Scramble the cards and put them face down in a pile.
- ♦ Take turns. Each person picks up a card, reads it, and decides if it is a FACT or an INFERENCE.
- ♦ Put the FACTS in one column and the INFERENCES in another.
- ♦ Share your answers with another pair or group.

✂ -

FACTS	INFERENCES
Victor Brashov is the owner of Crossroads Café.	Victor Brashov is too old to run a business.
Henry and Sara are 17-year olds.	Sara cares about Henry more than Henry cares about Sara.
Rosa is a cook.	Henry doesn't respect his parents.
Linda Blasco owns a laundromat.	Linda's laundromat will bring more customers to Crossroads Café.
Mr. and Mrs. Chang want Henry to date Chinese girls.	Both the Changs and the Graysons are prejudiced.
Edward wants to meet Karen Fong.	The Changs and the Graysons think Henry and Sara will get married.
Mr. and Mrs. Grayson went to Hong Kong.	Linda Blasco has good business sense.

ROLE-PLAY

HANDOUT 15-D

In this episode, everyone had a lot of opinions.

- ♦ Work with a partner.
- ♦ Read the situations below.
- ♦ Role-play one or more of the conversations or create your own role-play. Write it on the blank card.
- ♦ Share your role-play with the class.

Henry tells his mother about his dinner at the Graysons.	Mr. and Mrs. Chang talk about what happened at Crossroads Café.
Henry asks Jamal for advice.	Jamal tells Jihan what happened between Henry and Sara.
Rosa gives Henry advice.	Edward tells Henry about dinner with Mr. and Mrs. Fong.
Henry talks to Jess about intercultural dating.	Victor tells Nicolae about his new neighbor.
Sara talks to Henry after their parents meet at Crossroads Café.	Jess tells Carol about Victor's new neighbor.
Mr. and Mrs. Grayson talk about Henry after he leaves their house.	

It's lunchtime on a snowy, winter day. The employees at Crossroads Café are unhappy. The stove is not working, and there are very few customers.

Mr. Brashov is very worried about the stove, and he is angry, too. Jamal tries to fix the stove, but it is very old and needs a new part. Mr. Brashov says, "Maybe I need a new handyman." Jamal's feelings are very hurt.

Jess comes to the café. He usually comes in every day, but yesterday he didn't come. Jess joined a group at the Senior Citizens' Center. Now he plays chess there every morning.

Jess knows about the trouble with the stove. He tells Mr. Brashov to buy a new one. Mr. Brashov has a meeting tomorrow at a bank. He is going to apply for a loan to buy a new stove. Jess gives him advice about how to talk to the banker.

The next day Mr. Brashov goes to the bank. He follows Jess's advice, but it doesn't help. Mr. Littleton, the banker, thinks Mr. Brashov's expenses are too high. He will not approve a loan unless Mr. Brashov cuts his daily costs. One way to do this is to lay off some employees. Mr. Brashov needs to make more money if he wants a loan.

Later at the café, the employees want to know what happened at the bank. Mr. Brashov tells them. They discuss ways to get more customers, so Mr. Brashov can make more money. Henry offers to make flyers for a lunch special. He will put them around the neighborhood.

The next day, Crossroads Café has many customers. Mr. Brashov thanks Henry. But Henry didn't deliver any flyers. He overslept. Jess brought his group from the Senior Citizens' Center to the café for their morning coffee break.

Mr. Littleton from the bank enters the café. At first he is happy to see so many customers. Then he notices something. People are not eating. They are talking, reading the newspaper, playing cards, and sleeping. This is not the way to make more money. He tells Mr. Brashov to make changes fast!

Jess is in Mr. Brashov's office. Mr. Brashov is very sad. He is worried about the café and about the bank loan. Mr. Brashov tells Jess, "The banker thinks I am a fool. He will never give me a loan."

Nobody can find Jamal. Mr. Brashov was angry with Jamal because he couldn't fix the stove. Now Jamal hasn't come to work for two days. The employees wonder, "Is Jamal sick? Is he looking for a new job?"

Jess has another idea for a way to help Mr. Brashov. His seniors group will have lunch and play Bingo at Crossroads Café on Thursday. This time, everybody will order food!

When Mr. Littleton makes another surprise visit to Crossroads Café, he is happy to see so many customers eating. Maybe he will give Mr. Brashov a loan to buy a new stove.

Then Jamal comes to work. He is very dirty, but he is happy. He went to every junkyard in town, and he finally found the part to fix the stove. Mr. Brashov won't need a loan from the bank after all!

REPORTING INFORMATION

HANDOUT 16-A

Mr. Brashov had a meeting with a banker to talk about a loan. He told Jess about the meeting.

- ◆ Work with a partner.
- ◆ Each person write five questions on the blank cards below.
- ◆ Ask each other the questions and write the answers on your own paper.
- ◆ Work with another pair.
- ◆ Take turns reading each other the questions and reporting what your partner said.
- ◆ Use the two ways to report information from the *worktext*.

✂ -

INFORMATION GAP

HANDOUT 16-B

PARTNER A

Mr. Brashov went to a bank for a loan. But there are other places to get loans, too. With a partner look at these loan rates for a credit union.

♦ Ask and answer questions to find the missing information.

EXAMPLE: A: *What is the interest rate for a 12-month personal loan?*
B: *It's 11.25% APR.**

♦ Write the information in the blanks.

LOAN RATES	
Personal loans	**Auto Loans - Used Cars**
12 months	100% -1 year old/60 months . . . .
24 months 12.75%	90% - 2 years old/48 months 8.75%
25–36 months	90% -3 years old/42 months . . . .
Auto Loans - New Cars	**Home Equity Loans**
100% - 48 months 8.00%	60 months Fixed Rate 7.50%
100% - 60 months	120 months Fixed Rate . . . .
90% - 72 months 8.50%	180 months Variable Rate . . . . . Prime

* APR-Annual Percentage Rate

- -

PARTNER B

Mr. Brashov went to a bank for a loan. But there are other places to get loans, too. With a partner look at these loan rates for a credit union.

♦ Ask and answer questions to find the missing information.

EXAMPLE: B: *What is the interest rate for a 24-month personal loan?*
A: *It's 12.75% APR.**

♦ Write the information in the blanks.

LOAN RATES	
Personal loans	**Auto Loans - Used Cars**
12 months 11.75%	100% -1 year old/60 months 8.25%
24 months	90% - 2 years old/48 months . . . .
25–36 months 13.75%	90% -3 years old/42 months 8.75%
Auto Loans - New Cars	**Home Equity Loans**
100% - 48 months	60 months Fixed Rate . . . .
100% - 60 months 8.25%	120 months Fixed Rate . . . . Call
90% - 72 months	180 months Variable Rate

* APR-Annual Percentage Rate

SOLVE THE PROBLEM

HANDOUT 16-C

Mr. Brashov needs to improve his profits. In other words, he needs to make more money.

- ♦ Work with a partner or a small group.
- ♦ Read the ideas on the cards to help increase Mr. Brashov's profits.
- ♦ Write one or two more ideas on the blank cards.
- ♦ Together decide which ideas Mr. Brashov should use and which ideas he should ignore. Put them in two piles.
- ♦ Share your good ideas with the rest of the class. Explain why your ideas are good.

✂ -

Stay open longer hours.	Serve gourmet food and special drinks like espresso or latte.
Fire Jamal.	Redecorate.
Fire Henry.	Charge one price for breakfast meals, one price for lunches, and so on.
Reduce the number of items on the menu.	Advertise more and offer discounts to regular customers.
Serve only healthy foods—no salt, no fat, no sugar.	Offer senior citizen discounts.

INTERVIEW

HANDOUT 16-D

Jess surprises Mr. Brashov when he joins a group at the Senior Citizens' Center. Mr. Brashov wants to know why Jess wants to be with old people.

- ♦ Interview a partner about senior citizens.
- ♦ Write your partner's answers on the lines below.
- ♦ Share your interview with the rest of the class.

NAME:	INTERVIEWER:
1. To a 10-year old, 25 is old. What age is old to you?	
2. How will you know when you are old?	
3. Jess is retired. When do you plan to retire?	
4. What do you plan to do when you retire?	
5. Who do you think is older—Mr. Brashov or Jess? Why?	
6. Who is the oldest person you know? How old is this person?	
7. Does this person act old? Why or why not?	
8. Does this person have any problems because of his or her age?	
9. What are they? What are some things senior citizens shouldn't do?	
10. Many people over 75 years old live in retirement homes. Where will you live when you are 75?	

UNIT 17 UNITED WE STAND

Rosa is late for work. She is having problems with the water in her apartment. She has green cream on her face, and there is no water to wash her face. Finally, she cleans her face with mouthwash.

At Crossroads Café, Mr. Brashov is worried about Rosa because she is late. The restaurant needs its cook. Jess comes to the restaurant. His back hurts. Jess usually sits at the counter. Mr. Brashov tells him to sit on a chair at a table. The chair will be better for his back.

When Rosa arrives at work, she tells everyone about her water problems. Rosa tries to call the landlord, but she gets the answering machine. Jamal offers to help Rosa. He goes to her apartment after work to look at the pipes. The pipes are very old, and there is a leak. The sink needs a new faucet, too.

While Jamal is fixing the pipe under Rosa's sink, he accidentally breaks Rosa's radio. He takes the broken radio with him so he can fix it.

Rosa is very unhappy about the problems in her apartment building. She decides to write a letter to the building manager. Katherine tries to help. She thinks Rosa's letter is too nice. She gives Rosa suggestions to make the letter stronger. Katherine says, "Say the building is dirty. There are rats everywhere." Rosa is not sure Katherine's suggestions are good ideas.

Jess walks in the cafe. He sees Henry with a video camera. Henry tells Jess, "I'm making a documentary for my class. It's about work." Henry's teacher, Michael McAllister, is a reporter for a local TV station. Henry is filming everyone at the café.

A man comes to Crossroads Café. He is looking for Rosa. He is from the property management company for her building. Rosa did not pay her rent because her apartment needs repairs. Rosa says, "I need some repairs done. My bathroom faucet leaks." The man tells Rosa she must pay, so she gives him a check for the rent. Henry has his video camera, and he films Rosa and the man. This makes the man angry.

Katherine wants to help Rosa. She thinks Rosa should fight for changes in her building. Jess tells Rosa to ask the other tenants for help. Mr. Brashov tells Rosa to have a tenants' meeting at Crossroads Café. Everyone will help her. Jamal will make some signs, and Henry and Katherine will help set up the café for the meeting.

Henry brings Michael McAllister to the meeting. The tenants make a list of all the problems in their building. They elect Rosa president of their group. Then a stranger comes in. His name is Dr. Martinez, and he wants to help the tenants.

The next day at the restaurant, Henry turns on the TV and everyone watches the news. They see a story about the meeting at Crossroads Café. They find out about Dr. Martinez. He invested money in Rosa's building, and he is one of the owners. Before the meeting Dr. Martinez didn't know about the problems. Now he wants to help.

Dr. Martinez comes into the restaurant to see Rosa. He invites her to a meeting with his investment partners. They want to discuss the problems in Rosa's apartment building.

Henry gets his grade for the video. It's a B plus. He didn't get a better grade because his video was not about the topic—work.

MATCHING

HANDOUT 17-A

Work with a partner or a small group to match problems and complaints with solutions.

♦ Add two more complaints and solutions to the blank cards.
♦ Cut out the cards.
♦ Scramble them.
♦ Take turns reading the cards aloud.
♦ Match the problems or complaints with the solutions.
♦ Try to think of additional solutions for as many cards as you can.
♦ Share your solutions with the class.

PROBLEMS/COMPLAINTS	SOLUTIONS
Your paycheck has a mistake.	Tell your boss.
Your oven doesn't get hot.	Call an appliance repair person.
Your car won't start.	Call a service station.
Your phone doesn't work.	Ask a neighbor to use her phone.
A store advertised a CD player for $79.00, but the store doesn't have any in stock.	Ask for a raincheck.
Your car insurance increased $200.	Check into prices at other insurance companies.
The water in your toilet won't go down.	Call a plumber.
The milk you just bought is spoiled.	Return it and ask for a new gallon.

INFORMATION GAP

HANDOUT 17-B

PARTNER A

Directions: You are looking for a new apartment. The ads in the newspaper have many abbreviations. Ask your partner what the abbreviations mean. Complete the chart below.

EXAMPLE: A: *What does* **dlx** *mean?*
B: *It means* **deluxe.**
A: *Can you spell that?*
B: *Yes. d e l u x e.*

ABBREVIATION	WORD	ABBREVIATION	WORD
dlx		ht	heat
BR	bedroom	nr shpg	
incl		x-ways	expressways
appls	appliances	lrg	
prkg		a/c	air conditioning
sec	security	lndry facil	

- -

PARTNER B

Directions: You are looking for a new apartment. The ads in the newspaper have many abbreviations. Ask your partner what the abbreviations mean. Complete the chart below.

EXAMPLE: B: *What does* **ht** *mean?*
A: *It means* **heat.**
B: *Can you spell that?*
A: *Yes. h e a t.*

ABBREVIATION	WORD	ABBREVIATION	WORD
dlx	deluxe	ht	
BR		nr shpg	near shopping
incl	including	x-ways	
appls		lrg	large
prkg	parking	a/c	
sec		lndry facil	laundry facilities

Reproducible Handouts

BINGO

HANDOUT 17-C

B	I	N	G	O
AVL	DR	FLR	IMMAC	PVT
BA(S)	DIN RM	FRPL	KIT	REF
BLDG	D/W	**FREE SPACE**	LVG RM	SCHL
CPTG	ELEC	GAR	MO	STV
CRNR	ELEV	HW HT	NR	UTIL

100 ═══ Crossroads Café   United We Stand   © 1997 Heinle & Heinle Publishers

PROBLEM-SOLVING

HANDOUT 17-D

Everyone's home has problems.

- ♦ Make a list on the lines below of some problems in your home.
- ♦ Choose five problems and write them in the chart.
- ♦ Decide who can fix or solve each problem.
- ♦ Guess how much money it will cost to fix the problem (not all problems cost money to fix).
- ♦ Share your list with a partner or a small group and discuss the problems. Are your problems the same or different?
- ♦ Do your classmates agree with how much it will cost to fix the problems?

PROBLEMS: _____

_____

_____

_____

_____

_____

_____

_____

_____

PROBLEMS	HOW TO SOLVE	COST, IF ANY?

UNIT 18 OPPORTUNITY KNOCKS

Mr. Brashov is looking out the window. Jess asks, "Who are you looking for?" Mr. Brashov says, "Not who, what." Jess then says, "What?" But Mr. Brashov won't tell him. It's a surprise.

Jamal is trying to fix a toaster. He is very unhappy. When Mr. Brashov asks about the toaster, Jamal gets angry.

Mr. Brashov's surprise comes. It's a jukebox. Now Crossroads Café be Crossroads Musical Café! People like to listen to music. Music will bring more customers to Crossroads Café.

Mr. Brashov plugs in the jukebox. Nothing happens. No music. He calls for Jamal. He wants Jamal to fix the jukebox. But Jamal is still angry.

A customer is talking on a cellular phone. He is watching Jamal. He hears Jamal say, "I'm an engineer, not a jukebox engineer." When another customer asks Jamal about the jukebox, Jamal is rude to him. Before the customer with the cellular phone leaves, he gives Jamal his business card. The man's name is Rick Marshall. He owns a construction company. He tells Jamal to call him.

Jamal visits Rick Marshall, and he offers Jamal a job. Mr. Marshall needs a compliance engineer for his company. A compliance engineer makes sure the construction work matches the building plans. Jamal accepts the job.

At the café, Mr. Brashov wants Jamal to make a sign for the café about the jukebox. But Jamal quits his job at Crossroads Café.

Jamal is at the construction company. Mr. Marshall shows Jamal around the job site and introduces him to other employees. Joe Cassidy, a project manager, gives Mr. Marshall an envelope.

Jamal is alone in the construction office at night. The phone rings. He goes to Mr. Marshall's desk to answer the phone. It's Jihan. While Jamal is talking to his wife, he spills some coffee. It falls on an envelope with computer disks.

Jamal is worried about the disks. He wipes the coffee off the disks. Then he puts a disk in the computer to check it for damage. Jamal sees something on the disk. It's a crack in one of the beams for a building at the construction site.

At the café, Mr. Brashov decides to put two ads in the newspaper—one ad is for a handyman and the other ad is for the jukebox. He wants to sell it. The jukebox is too much trouble!

Jamal talks to Mr. Marshall. He wants Jamal to sign some papers. Jamal doesn't want to sign them. He knows the building is not safe. Mr. Marshall gives Jamal an envelope with many one hundred dollar bills in it. It's a bribe to get Jamal to sign the papers. After Mr. Marshall leaves the office, Jamal picks up the telephone. He calls the Department of Building and Safety.

Mr. Brashov is interviewing applicants for the handyman job. He is having no luck finding a new handyman. Then Jamal walks in. He says, "I heard you are looking for a handyman. I'm here to apply for the job."

Jamal is working for Crossroads Café again—not Crossroads Musical Café. Mr. Brashov sold the jukebox.

CARD GAME

HANDOUT 18-A

Mr. Brashov bought a jukebox for Crossroads Café to attract more customers. Which do you prefer? A quiet restaurant or a restaurant with music?

♦ Work with a partner or a small group.
♦ Write two more choices on the blank cards.
♦ Cut the cards on the lines, scramble them, and put them face down in a pile.
♦ One person turns over a card.
♦ The person reads the card aloud, says which thing she prefers and gives a reason.

    EXAMPLE: *I prefer hot dogs. Hot dogs are cheaper than hamburgers.*

Don't forget to use **er** or **more** in your sentences!

----

hot dogs or hamburgers?	game shows or situation comedies?
cooking or cleaning?	country music or rock and roll?
running or walking?	houses or apartments?
new cars or used cars?	escalators or elevators?
cities or suburbs?	glasses or contact lenses?
dogs or cats?	long hair or short hair?
airplanes or trains?	Italian food or Chinese food?

HANDOUT 18-B

When Rick Marshall met Jamal, he gave him a business card. Then he told Jamal to call him. Jamal called, and Mr. Marshall offered him a job.

♦ Work with a partner.
♦ Read the business cards below.
♦ Write a reason why you would call the person on each card.
♦ Select two cards and role-play conversations.
♦ Share one role-play with the class.

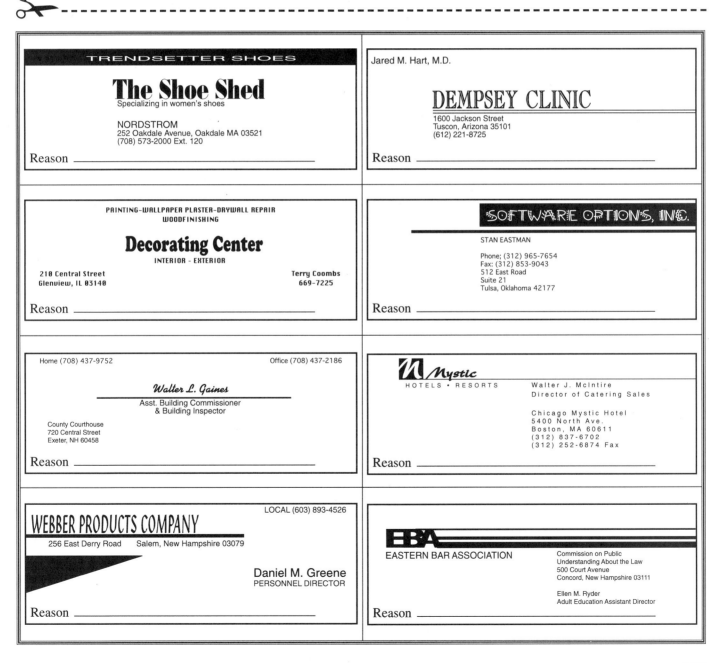

TRENDSETTER SHOES

The Shoe Shed
Specializing in women's shoes

NORDSTROM
252 Oakdale Avenue, Oakdale MA 03521
(708) 573-2000 Ext. 120

Reason _____

Jared M. Hart, M.D.

DEMPSEY CLINIC
1600 Jackson Street
Tuscon, Arizona 35101
(612) 221-8725

Reason _____

PAINTING-WALLPAPER PLASTER-DRYWALL REPAIR
WOODFINISHING

Decorating Center
INTERIOR - EXTERIOR

210 Central Street
Glenview, IL 03140

Terry Coombs
669-7225

Reason _____

SOFTWARE OPTIONS, INC.

STAN EASTMAN

Phone: (312) 965-7654
Fax: (312) 853-9043
512 East Road
Suite 21
Tulsa, Oklahoma 42177

Reason _____

Home (708) 437-9752   Office (708) 437-2186

Walter L. Gaines
Asst. Building Commissioner
& Building Inspector

County Courthouse
720 Central Street
Exeter, NH 60458

Reason _____

Mystic
HOTELS • RESORTS

Walter J. McIntire
Director of Catering Sales

Chicago Mystic Hotel
5400 North Ave.
Boston, MA 60611
(312) 837-6702
(312) 252-6874 Fax

Reason _____

WEBBER PRODUCTS COMPANY
256 East Derry Road   Salem, New Hampshire 03079

LOCAL (603) 893-4526

Daniel M. Greene
PERSONNEL DIRECTOR

Reason _____

EBA
EASTERN BAR ASSOCIATION

Commission on Public
Understanding About the Law
500 Court Avenue
Concord, New Hampshire 03111

Ellen M. Ryder
Adult Education Assistant Director

Reason _____

SOLVE THE PROBLEM

HANDOUT 18-C

Jamal's boss tried to bribe him to sign some papers. But Jamal didn't accept the bribe. He called the Department of Building and Safety; then he quit his job. Do you know people who have had problems like Jamal?

- ◆ Work with a partner or in a small group.
- ◆ Read the problem cards.
- ◆ Write one more problem on the blank card.
- ◆ Choose one or two problems to discuss.
- ◆ Make one or two suggestions to solve the problem.
- ◆ Share the suggestions with the class.

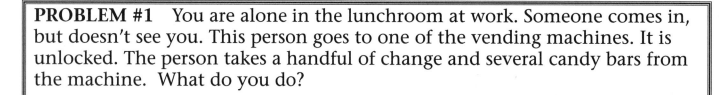

PROBLEM #1 You are alone in the lunchroom at work. Someone comes in, but doesn't see you. This person goes to one of the vending machines. It is unlocked. The person takes a handful of change and several candy bars from the machine. What do you do?

PROBLEM #2 You are shopping at a department store. It's very busy. There is only one clerk, and there are six customers behind you in line. When you get home, you review your bill. The clerk charged you twice for one sale item. She didn't charge you for another item. What do you do?

PROBLEM #3 You have new neighbors, a single father and his three children. The children are 4-, 6-, and 8-years old. You notice the father leaves the children home alone several times a week at night. What do you do?

PROBLEM #4 Your house is for sale. The real estate agent asks if there are any problems with the house. Should you tell the real estate agent the roof leaks? You didn't fix the roof, but you painted the ceiling so the water marks don't show. What do you do?

PROBLEM # 5

INTERVIEW

HANDOUT 18-D

Most paychecks show employees' benefits.

♦ Read the paycheck below.

♦ Work with a partner and answer the questions.

♦ Write your answers on the lines.

Builders Barn	Builders Barn, Inc. 712 Main Street San Antonio, Texas 78228			CHECK NO: 328537 CHECK DATE: 10/27/96 PERIOD ENDING: 10/22/96 PAY FREQUENCY: BIWEEKLY		
Marcelo Sala 1453 South St. Allenvale, IL 60139	SSN: 332-00-5807 EXEMPTIONS: FED: 00 STATE: 00 TAX ADJ: FED: STATE:	NUMBER: 0332645807 STATE CODE: PRI: IL SEC: SDI/UC ALT:		TAX STATUS: SINGLE LOCAL CODE: LOC1: LOC2: LOC3: LOCAL ALT: BASE RATE: 7.9000		

HOURS AND EARNINGS				TAXES AND DEDUCTIONS			SPECIAL INFORMATION
DESCRIPTION	CURRENT HOURS/UNITS EARNINGS		Y-T-D HOURS/UNITS EARNINGS	DESCRIPTION	CURRENT AMOUNT	Y-T-D AMOUNT	
REGULAR	64.00	505.60		SO SEC TAX	39.18	673.71	
VACATION	8.00	63.20		MEDICARE TAX	9.16	157.56	
BIRTHDAY	8.00	63.20		FED INC TAX	79.80	1314.89	
				PRI-STATE TAX	18.96	325.94	
TOTAL H/E	80.00	832.00		TOTAL TAXES	147.10	2472.10	
PRE-TAX ITEMS				AFTER-TAX DEDUCTIONS			
				CASH		202.96	
TOTAL PRE-TAX				EMPLOYEE CLUB		21.00	
TOTAL	80.00	632.00		TOTAL PER DED		223.96	
GROSS		PRE-TAX	TAXABLE WAGES	LESS TAXES	LESS DED	EQ NET PAY	
CURRENT	632.00	.00	632.00	147.10	.00	484.90	
Y-T-D	10866.32	.00	10866.32	2472.10	223.96	8170.26	

1. What is Marcelo's gross salary? _____

2. How much does he pay to Social Security? _____

3. How much does he pay for health insurance? _____

4. How many sick days does he have? _____

5. How many vacation days does he have? _____

6. Are there any other deductions for benefits? What are they? _____

_____

Write one or two more questions to ask a partner about this paycheck.

♦ Interview each other about job benefits in your native countries.

♦ Write your partner's answers on the spaces below.

♦ Share the information with the class.

INTERVIEW	NAME:	NATIVE COUNTRY:
1. Do paychecks have deductions for government-funded pensions?		
2. Do paychecks have deductions for health insurance?		
3. Do paychecks show vacation and sick days?		
4. What other benefits are on paychecks?		
5. What other deductions are on paychecks?		

UNIT 19   THE PEOPLE'S CHOICE

Mr. Brashov is unhappy. There is construction in front of Crossroads Café, and it is keeping customers away. Mr. Brashov calls the city office to complain, but he can't find anyone to speak to.

A young Middle Eastern man enters the café. He tells Mr. Brashov, "People are putting pieces of wood on the street in front of your café." Mr. Brashov doesn't know the man, but he looks familiar.

Jamal enters. He asks, "Has anyone seen my cousin?" The young Middle Eastern man enters the café again. He's Jamal's cousin Hassan. Jamal introduces him to everyone. Hassan likes Rosa very much. Hassan is in the United States to learn English. He wants to be a tour guide in Egypt.

Later that morning, Jess comes to the café. He shows his water bill to Mr. Brashov. Jess's bill for one month of water is $30,000. Jess called the city to complain, but nobody helped him.

Both Jess and Mr. Brashov are unhappy with the city. Mr. Brashov tells Jess to run for city council.

Later at home, Jess talks to his wife, Carol, about Mr. Brashov's idea. Carol thinks it's a good idea, too. She says to Jess, "You could be the *people's choice.*"

Jess decides to run for city council. Crossroads Café becomes his campaign headquarters. There are posters and flyers in the café for Jess Washington, the "People's Choice." But nobody knows Jess, and his name is not mentioned in the newspaper polls.

Mr. Brashov has an idea. He wants Jess to make speeches at Crossroads Café while people are eating. Only one customer is interested in Jess's first speech. His name is Dan Miller.

Dan Miller tells his boss, Mr. Comstock, about Jess. Andrew Comstock is a businessman. He wants to help elect someone to the city council. If Andrew Comstock helps Jess, Jess will help him. Dan brings Mr. Comstock to the café to see Jess.

Dan Miller and Mr. Comstock have a lot of ideas to help Jess. They change his looks, and they give him ideas for speeches. One day, Jess is sitting at a table in Crossroads Café, and nobody recognizes him. Jess is wearing a toupee!

Carol is not happy with the new Jess. She will not vote for him. She doesn't like Mr. Comstock either. He thinks more about money than people.

Jess is giving another speech at Crossroads Café. When Jess sees Carol, he changes his speech. He takes off his toupee. He is the old Jess, and Mr. Comstock is very angry. He won't help Jess anymore.

Hassan is getting ready to return to Egypt. He tries to give Rosa a goat. This is a marriage proposal custom in Egypt. Rosa is very surprised. She likes Hassan, but she doesn't want to marry him.

Election night arrives. Everyone is at Crossroads Café. They are waiting to hear the election results. The phone rings, and Katherine answers it. Jess has 18,706 votes and Tom Johansen has 19,706 votes. Jess didn't win the election, but he didn't lose either.

HANDOUT 19-A

Jess told voters, "I promise you I'll be the best councilman this city has ever had." What other promises do the people in the story make?

♦ Work with a partner or in a small group.
♦ Cut the cards on the lines.
♦ Write more names on the blank cards.
♦ Scramble the cards and put them face down in a pile.
♦ Take turns. One person turns over a card and makes a promise. The other person asks questions about the promise.
♦ Share one or two promises with the class.

Jess to Carol	Mr. Brashov to Jess
Carol to Jess	Dan Miller to Jess
Andrew Comstock to Jess	Henry to Mr. Brashov
Rosa to Katherine	Jamal to Mr. Brashov

INTERVIEW

HANDOUT 19-B

Jess and Mr. Brashov had complaints about their city. Jess got a $30,000 water bill. Mr. Brashov called the city to complain about construction traffic. Are there problems in your community?

♦ Interview a partner.
♦ Ask questions about his or her community.
♦ Circle the numbers in the chart and write comments on the lines.
♦ Share the information with a small group.
♦ Report the groups' information to the class.

NAME: _____ COMMUNITY: _____
INTERVIEWER: _____
How satisfied are you with your community? Circle the numbers. Tell how you feel and explain why.

	Very Satisfied	Satisfied	Dissatisfied	Very Dissatisfied
Housing	1	2	3	4
Transportation	1	2	3	4
Cleanliness	1	2	3	4
Police Protection	1	2	3	4
Schools	1	2	3	4
Library	1	2	3	4
Taxes	1	2	3	4
Parks	1	2	3	4

Other:

Overall rating:

Comments: _____
_____
_____
_____

DIALOGUE

HANDOUT 19-C

Jess complains about his water bill. His friends at Crossroads Café tell him to run for city council. His wife, Carol, also thinks it's a good idea.

- ♦ Work with a partner.
- ♦ Read the dialogue cards below.
- ♦ While you watch the video, put the conversation in order.
- ♦ Share with another pair. Is the order of the cards the same?

✂ ---

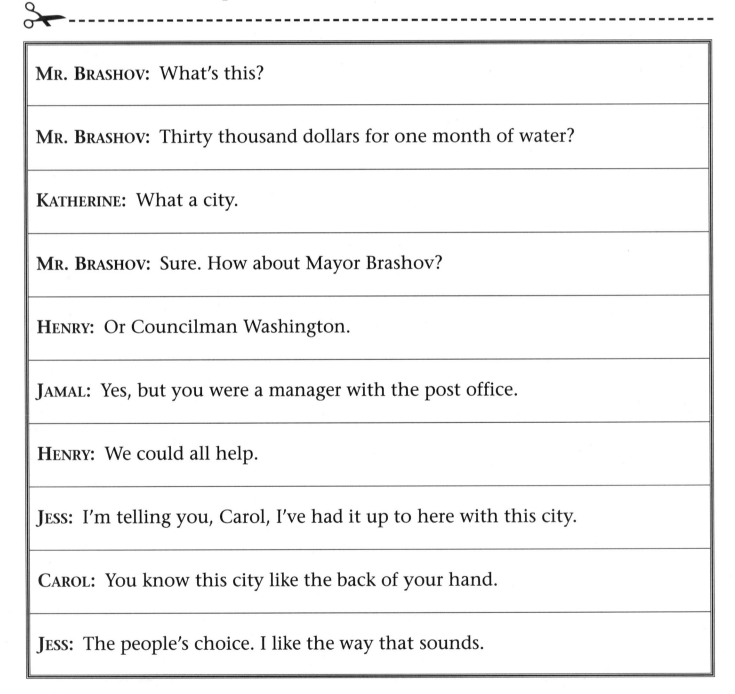

MR. BRASHOV: What's this?
MR. BRASHOV: Thirty thousand dollars for one month of water?
KATHERINE: What a city.
MR. BRASHOV: Sure. How about Mayor Brashov?
HENRY: Or Councilman Washington.
JAMAL: Yes, but you were a manager with the post office.
HENRY: We could all help.
JESS: I'm telling you, Carol, I've had it up to here with this city.
CAROL: You know this city like the back of your hand.
JESS: The people's choice. I like the way that sounds.

WHAT DO YOU KNOW?

HANDOUT 19-D

Jess decided to run for city council.

- ◆ Ask your classmates the questions below.
- ◆ Write their answers in the chart below.
- ◆ Ask each classmate only one question.
- ◆ Share the answers with the class.

QUESTION	ANSWER
1. Who is the president of the United States?	
2. Who is the vice president?	
3. When is Election Day?	
4. How many senators are there in the United States?	
5. How many representatives are there?	
6. Who are the senators in your state?	
7. Who is your representative?	
8. Who is the governor of your state?	
9. What is the state capitol?	
10. Who is the mayor of your city?	
11. What is the legal voting age in the United States?	
12. What is the national anthem?	
13. Have you ever campaigned for anyone? Who?	
14. Have you ever met a politician? Who?	
15. Have you ever run for a political office?	

It's Monday morning. Rosa and Katherine are talking about the weekend. Rosa begins to tell Katherine about a guest teacher. But she is interrupted.

Bill comes to say good-bye to Katherine. He is going to a conference in Chicago. Katherine reminds Bill, "Don't forget my bear." Katherine collects stuffed animals.

Mr. Brashov asks Rosa about lunch. He wants to have a special dessert with lunch because Mr. Shuster, his landlord, is coming to talk about a new lease.

Mr. Shuster tells Mr. Brashov, "You have a wonderful restaurant." Then he gives Mr. Brashov some bad news. The taxes have gone up, and he will probably have to increase the rent.

A man comes into the café. Rosa recognizes him. It's her guest teacher, Andrew Collins. Rosa is very nervous when she talks to Andrew Collins. She tells him about the lunch special. But Mr. Collins doesn't want lunch. He wants to ask Rosa for a favor. Mr. Collins needs a translator for a meeting at his home. Rosa agrees to help him.

Mr. Shuster finishes lunch. Mr. Brashov is nervous about the new lease. He wants to meet with Mr. Shuster and his accountant. But Mr. Shuster is very busy. His son, Stuart, is coming home from school next week. Mr. Shuster's son has to write a school paper about how to run a small business. When Mr. Brashov hears this, he offers to help Stuart.

Rosa is at Andrew Collins' apartment. The furniture is very expensive, and there are a lot of antiques and artwork. One guest, Libby Flanders, is rude to Rosa. She asks Rosa her opinion about a painting. Then she tells Rosa, "You do not belong here."

A few days later at work, Rosa is studying. She's trying to learn about art, music, and wine so she can talk to Andrew and his friends.

Mr. Shuster brings Stuart to Crossroads Café. Mr. Brashov is very surprised. Stuart looks like an 11- or 12-year old. But he dresses and talks like an adult.

Rosa is at Andrew's apartment again. Now she has blond hair, and she talks about art and wine. Andrew is surprised.

At the café, Stuart makes Jamal angry. Jamal and Henry take Stuart out of the café. This worries Mr. Brashov. He calls after them, "You aren't going to do anything violent, are you?"

When Jamal and Henry bring Stuart back to the café, he looks different. His hair is uncombed, and he is dirty. He was playing soccer with Henry and Jamal. Then Mr. Shuster comes in. He's happy about the way Stuart looks. Stuart looks like a kid!

Rosa goes to Andrew's apartment. Andrew is going to Switzerland. Rosa is very disappointed. She enjoyed her dates with Andrew, but they were not dates to him. They were business.

Back at the café, there is one more surprise. Bill is back from Chicago. He kisses Katherine and gives her a big box. Inside, there are two presents, a stuffed bear and an engagement ring.

GIVE ADVICE

HANDOUT 20-A

People use **should** to give advice to their friends, families, neighbors, and coworkers. People use **had better** for strong advice or warnings.

- Work with a partner or in a small group.
- Cut out the cards, scramble them, and put them face down in a pile.
- One person turns over a card and reads it aloud.
- The other people in the group, give advice about the topic or person on the card—orally or in writing.

EXAMPLE: **HENRY—TABLES**
Henry should clean the tables as soon as the customers leave.

HENRY—TABLES	**KATHERINE—BILL**	**MR. SHUSTER—RENT**
JAMAL—BABYSITTER	**BILL—BEAR**	**STUART—PLAY**
MR. BRASHOV—ORDER SUPPLIES	**ANDREW—ROSA**	**RICARDO—ENGLISH**
ROSA—HAIR	**LIBBY—ROSA**	**ROSA-MAID**

INFORMATION GAP

HANDOUT 20-B

PARTNER A

Rosa and Katherine want to go to the movies. What time should they go and what should they see?

♦ Work with a partner.

♦ Ask and answer questions about the movie schedules below.
   EXAMPLE: A: *How much are the movies at <u>Glendale Square</u>?*
            B: *<u>$1.00</u>*

♦ Write the missing information in the blanks.

♦ Together agree on a movie and time.

GLENDALE SQUARE _____ All Shows 847-921-8564	WESTGATE $1.00 til 6 P.M. $1.75 after 6 P.M.	NORTH AVENUE
Tall Women _____ 1:30, 4:45, 7:20 **Helicopter** (PG-13) _____, 9:50 **Going to L.A.** (R) 1:20, 5:10, _____	**Cold** (R) _____ only **Going to L.A.** _____ 2:15, _____, 7:00 **Peaches** (PG) _____, 7:20, 9:30	**Tall Women** _____ 2:00, 4:15, 7:00 **The Journey** (R) 2:00, 4:00, _____, 9:00 **Falling Asleep** (R) 5:15, 7:10, 9:10

 -

PARTNER B

Rosa and Katherine want to go to the movies. What time should they go and what should they see?

♦ Work with a partner.

♦ Ask and answer questions about the movie schedules below.
   EXAMPLE: B: *What are the times for <u>Tall Women</u>?*
            A: *1:30, <u>4:45</u>, and 7:20.*

♦ Write the missing information in the blanks.

♦ Together agree on a movie and time.

GLENDALE SQUARE $1.00 All Shows 847-921-8564	WESTGATE til 6 P.M. $1.75 after 6 P.M.	NORTH AVENUE $2
Tall Women (R) 1:30, _____, 7:20 **Helicopter** _____ 7:30, _____ **Going to L.A.** (R) _____, 5:10, 7:40	**Cold** _____ 7:30 only **Going to L.A.** (R) _____, 4:40, 7:00 **Peaches** (PG) 3:15, 7:20, _____	**Tall Women** (R) 2:00, 4:15, _____ **The Journey** (R) 2:00, 4:00, 7:00, 9:00 **Falling Asleep** _____ 5:15, _____, 9:10

SOLVE THE PROBLEM

HANDOUT 20-C

Mr. Shuster worries about his son, Stuart. He acts like an adult, not a child. It is hard work to raise a child.

- ◆ Work with a partner or in a small group.
- ◆ Read and discuss the problems below.
- ◆ Write one more problem on the blank card.
- ◆ Give the problem to another pair or group to discuss.
- ◆ Share your suggestions with the class.

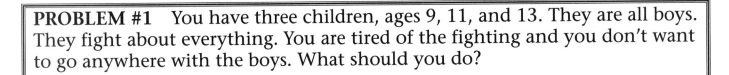

PROBLEM #1 You have three children, ages 9, 11, and 13. They are all boys. They fight about everything. You are tired of the fighting and you don't want to go anywhere with the boys. What should you do?

PROBLEM #2 Your daughter is 13-years old. You do not like her friends. When they come to your house, they never even say hello. Your daughter is not doing her homework, and she lies to you about everything. You also think she is stealing from your wallet. What should you do?

PROBLEM #3 Your daughter is 16-years old. She got her driver's license one month ago. So far, she has had one accident and one ticket for speeding. The cost of your car insurance is going up. You are worried. What should you do?

PROBLEM #4 You have a 3-year old boy. He is afraid of everything. He wants the lights on when he sleeps and he wants you to sleep with him. He doesn't want to play outside because he is afraid of spiders, bees, and dogs. When dogs bark, he cries. He follows you everywhere, and he wants you to hold him all of the time. You are tired and worried. What should you do?

PROBLEM # 5

INTERVIEW

HANDOUT 20-D

How are ideas about raising children in your native country different from ideas in the United States?

- ♦ Interview a partner about parenting.
- ♦ Ask the questions below and put checkmarks in the correct columns.
- ♦ Write four more questions and ask them, too.
- ♦ Share the answers with the class.

	IN MY COUNTRY		IN THE UNITED STATES	
	YES	NO	YES	NO
1. Do people usually have more than two children?				
2. Do parents want boys more than girls?				
3. Do parents hire babysitters for their children?				
4. Do children go to preschool?				
5. Do children have a lot of expensive toys?				
6. Do children have chores to do at home?				
7. Do children get money for doing chores at home?				
8. Do children have a lot of time to play with other children?				
9.				
10.				
11.				
12.				

WALLS AND BRIDGES

Crossroads Café is closed. Mr. Brashov and Rosa are planning menus for the week. María Hernandez comes into the café. She is bringing dinner to her father, César. César is the evening janitor at Crossroads Café. César is also a tailor, and he owns a tailoring shop in the neighborhood.

María shows a photo to Rosa. It is from Big Sister Week at María's school. Rosa is María's "Big Sister," and Rosa is very proud of María. She won a science award at school.

The next day, Mr. Brashov and Jess are playing chess. Jess asks Mr. Brashov about his citizenship exam. Mr. Brashov is studying, but it is very hard. Jess offers to help Mr. Brashov study. But Mr. Brashov refuses Jess's help.

María's teacher, Chris Scanlon comes in the café. She is looking for Rosa. Chris is worried about María because she isn't coming to school anymore. Chris doesn't speak Spanish so she asks Rosa to talk to María's parents.

Rosa goes to the Hernandez's tailoring shop. César is pinning the hem of Rosa's skirt. María is surprised to see Rosa. Rosa tells María about Mrs. Scanlon's visit. María is uncomfortable. Her father doesn't want her to talk to Rosa.

Finally, Rosa asks César, "Why isn't María in school?" César needs María to work in his shop. Rosa is very angry when she hears César's reasons. She wants to do something to help María.

María comes to Crossroads Café to say hello to Rosa. Henry tells María about the work-study program. Students go to school for half a day and work for half a day. Rosa thinks this would be a good way for María to continue school.

Rosa and Mrs. Scanlon go to the tailoring shop. They want to tell Mr. Hernandez about the work-study program. He is not interested. María will get married and have children. She does not need an education.

Mr. Brashov's citizenship test is tomorrow. He can't remember anything. Jess and Katherine offer to help him study. Mr. Brashov finally accepts their help. He also asks Jess to go with him to the interview.

The next day, Mr. Brashov is very excited. He passed the citizenship test. Everyone congratulates him.

Mr. Hernandez comes into the café. Mr. Brashov tells him the news about his citizenship test. Mr. Brashov is very happy, but he is also a little sad. Mr. Brashov's daughter doesn't know about her father's good news. They had a fight, and they don't speak to each other. Mr. Hernandez thinks about Mr. Brashov's problems with his daughter. Mr. Brashov talks about his daughter to Mr. Hernandez.

María comes in the café. She brings her father's dinner. César asks María, "Is it terrible to be a tailor?" María says, "No Papa, not for you." But María doesn't want to be a tailor. She wants to do other things. She wants an education.

Mr. Hernandez surprises María. He finally agrees to talk to Mrs. Scanlon about the work-study program. María can go back to school.

ROLE-PLAY

HANDOUT 21-A

Jess offered to help Mr. Brashov study several times. Finally Mr. Brashov accepted Jess's help—the night before his citizenship test.

♦ Work with a partner or in a small group.
♦ Cut the cards, scramble them, and put them face down in a pile.
♦ Person **A** turns over a card and reads it aloud to Person **B**. They follow the directions on the card.

EXAMPLE:

> *OPEN CAR DOOR*
> A: *offer help*
> B: *say no*

A: *Would you like me to open the car door?*
B: *No, thanks. I can do it myself.*

 -

TURN OFF THE COMPUTER A: ask for help B: say yes	ANSWER THE PHONE A: offer help B: say no	GIVE A CUSTOMER A MENU A: ask for help B: say yes
PIN UP THIS HEM A: ask for help B: say no	MAKE A FOOD DELIVERY A: offer help B: say yes	WATCH THE KIDS AFTER SCHOOL A: ask for help B: say yes
TAKE A PICTURE A: offer help B: say no	LOCK THE FRONT DOOR A: ask for help B: say yes	PUT THE CLOSED SIGN IN THE WINDOW A: ask for help B: say no
FIX THE CHAIR A: offer help B: say yes	FILL OUT THE WORK-STUDY FORM A: ask for help B: say yes	OPEN THE DOOR A: ask for help B: say no

ROLE-PLAY

HANDOUT 21-B

María stopped going to school because she had to work in her family's tailoring shop. Mrs. Scanlon, one of her teachers, tried to help María.

- ♦ Work with a partner or in a small group.
- ♦ Read the problems below.
- ♦ For each problem, write suggestions for parents and teachers on the lines.
- ♦ Write one more problem and give it to another pair or group to write suggestions.
- ♦ Role-play one of the problems for the class.

#1 Cecilio is in kindergarten. He hits the other children and yells at them. He has no friends.	#2 Jin is in 4th grade. He doesn't like math. He doesn't know his multiplication tables.
PARENTS TEACHER	PARENTS TEACHER
_____ _____	_____ _____
_____ _____	_____ _____
_____ _____	_____ _____
_____ _____	_____ _____
_____ _____	_____ _____
#3 Larissa is in 8th grade. She was an A student. Now she gets Cs and Ds, and she doesn't want to go to school.	#4 _____ _____ _____
PARENTS TEACHER	PARENTS TEACHER
_____ _____	_____ _____
_____ _____	_____ _____
_____ _____	_____ _____
_____ _____	_____ _____
_____ _____	_____ _____

DIALOGUE

HANDOUT 21-C

Mr. Brashov and Mr. Hernandez talk about citizenship and their daughters. Why does Mr. Hernandez change his mind about the work-study program?

♦ Work with a partner.
♦ Read the dialogue cards below.
♦ While you watch **Story Clip #3**, put the conversation in order.
♦ Share with another pair. Is the order of the cards the same?

✂ -

Mr. Brashov: César, stay a minute.
César: Congratulations. You must be very proud.
Mr. Brashov: We don't speak, we don't visit.
Mr. Brashov: You still have your daughter with you.
Mr. Brashov: Would you insist that he quit school?
Mr. Brashov: But this is America.
César: You think I should allow this work-study?
César: Is being a tailor so terrible?
María: I love you, Papa, and I respect you.
César: Tomorrow, we will talk to Mrs. Scanlon.

UNSCRAMBLE AND SEQUENCE

HANDOUT 21-D

Mr. Brashov wants to become a U.S. citizen. Here are the steps.

- ◆ Work with a partner or in a small group.
- ◆ Cut the cards.
- ◆ Put the scrambled words into sentences.
- ◆ Add capital letters and periods.
- ◆ Put the sentences into order according to what Mr. Brashov said first, second, third, and so on.
- ◆ Share your sentences with another group.

✂ -

have	three	photographer	take	a
color	yourself	of	photos	

your	get	fingerprints	taken
police	a	at	station

get	from	citizenship	application	a
and	Naturalization	the	Immigration	Service

the	out	fill	form	and	with
it	send	$95.00	to	INS	

interview	for	the	prepare	and
study	for	test	citizenship	the

interview	to	the	report
with	documents	supporting	your

and	the	United	civics
history	take	States	test

test	the	interview	and	pass	and
the	to	go	ceremony	in	swearing

A man is sitting on a bench outside Crossroads Café. He is reading the newspaper. The man needs to shave, and his clothes are dirty.

Henry looks out the window and sees the man. Katherine says, "He's been out there since this morning. Should we do something?" Jess says, "No. He's just reading the paper."

Mr. Brashov is reading a list from Jamal. Jamal is going on vacation so he is leaving some instructions for Mr. Brashov. Jamal and his daughter, Azza, will meet Jihan on a business trip.

Katherine looks out the window again and sees the man on the bench. She asks, "Mr. Brashov, have you noticed that man sitting out front?" She asks Rosa about the man, too. Only Katherine is worried about the man.

Finally, Katherine opens the door for Jess. The man is at the door. His hands are in his pockets. Katherine asks the man, "What do you want?" He says, "I need something to eat." The man comes into the café. Katherine thinks the man is a robber with a gun. She tells Rosa to make a turkey sandwich for him, quickly.

The man is very nervous. He starts to take his hands out of his pockets. Everyone puts their hands in the air. The man is very confused. He is not a robber. He is just hungry.

The lights go out in the café. The man helps Mr. Brashov fix the lights. Then he introduces himself. His name is Frank. He has not worked for 18 months. Mr. Brashov and Jess want to help him. Katherine does not. She doesn't trust Frank.

The next day at the café, Mr. Brashov is trying to fix a lock. Then Frank comes in and offers to help. Mr. Brashov asks Frank to fill in for Jamal. Frank is the new handyman for a week.

Jess is having car problems. Frank offers to look at Jess's car. Frank used to be a mechanic. When Jess tries to pay Frank, Frank refuses the money.

Jess wants to help Frank. Jess used to work at the post office. He knows about a job there, so he sets up a job interview for Frank.

Frank has good job skills, but he doesn't do well on job interviews. Jess and Mr. Brashov help Frank get ready for the interview. They pretend to interview him. Henry types his resumé. Rosa gives him a shave, and Jess gives him some clothes. Finally, Frank is ready for his job interview.

Jess's friend, Marty, comes to Crossroads Café to interview Frank. Frank is very nervous. He gives Marty his resumé. They talk for a little bit, but then Frank gets up and walks away.

Frank feels very bad. He disappointed Jess and Mr. Brashov. Katherine talks to Frank. She tells him, "I know how you feel. When I came to Crossroads Café, I was very nervous, too."

Katherine gives Frank some advice. She tells him to imagine the interviewer is in his underwear. Then Frank won't be so nervous.

Frank gets another chance to interview with Marty. This time he follows Katherine's advice, and he gets the job!

CARD GAME

HANDOUT 22-A

With a partner, practice asking for permission.

- ♦ Cut the cards and scramble them. Put them face down in a pile.
- ♦ One person turns over a card and shows it to the partner.
- ♦ The first person starts the conversation.
- ♦ The second person turns over the next card and starts the conversation.
- ♦ Share one conversation with the rest of the class.

A: Can I use your car? B: Yes, but . . . A: B:	A: Can I look at your homework? B: I'm sorry, but . . . A: B:
A: Can I . . . ? B: Yes, . . . A: B:	A: Can I . . . ? B: I'm sorry, but, . . . A: B:
A: May I use the telephone? B: Yes, but . . . A: B:	A: May I turn up the radio? B: No. I'm sorry, but . . . A: B:
A: May I . . . ? B: Yes, . . . A: B:	A: May I . . . ? B: No . . . A: B:

A: Do you mind if I miss class
    next week?
B: No, but . . .
A:
B:
	A: Do you mind if I go out with
	    some friends tonight?
	B: Yes, I do. I have . . .
	A:
	B:

A: Do you mind if I . . . ? B: No, . . . A: B:	A: Do you mind if I . . . ? B: Yes . . . A: B:

PUT IT IN ORDER

HANDOUT 22-B

Frank hasn't had a job for 18 months. Mr. Brashov, Jess, Katherine, Henry, and Rosa help him get ready for his job interview.

- ◆ Work with a partner.
- ◆ Cut the cards and scramble them. Put them face up.
- ◆ Put the cards in order while you watch the video clip.
- ◆ Share the order of the cards with another pair.
- ◆ Is the order of the cards the same? Discuss any differences.

✂ -

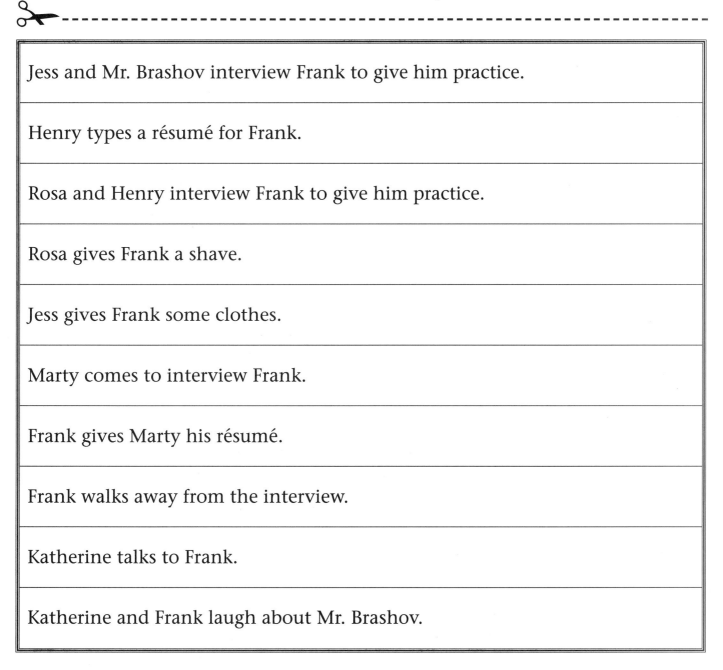

| Jess and Mr. Brashov interview Frank to give him practice. |
| Henry types a résumé for Frank. |
| Rosa and Henry interview Frank to give him practice. |
| Rosa gives Frank a shave. |
| Jess gives Frank some clothes. |
| Marty comes to interview Frank. |
| Frank gives Marty his résumé. |
| Frank walks away from the interview. |
| Katherine talks to Frank. |
| Katherine and Frank laugh about Mr. Brashov. |

INTERVIEW

HANDOUT 22-C

At first, Katherine didn't like Frank. She didn't want to help him. Then she changed her mind.

- ◆ Read the sentences below.
- ◆ Put checks in the opinion columns.
- ◆ Write two more sentences about the video.
- ◆ Work with a partner.
- ◆ Share your opinions.
- ◆ Did you change any of your opinions after you discussed them? Which ones?

OPINIONS

	AGREE	DON'T KNOW	DISAGREE
1. Mr. Brashov has a kind heart.			
2. Katherine is afraid of Frank.			
3. Frank wants Jamal's job.			
4. Jamal is jealous of his wife's job.			
5. Jamal will never go on another business trip with Jihan.			
6. Jamal should have left Azza at home with a babysitter.			
7. Frank won't keep his new job for long.			
8. Anyone can find a job.			
9.			
10.			

MATCH UP

HANDOUT 22-D

There are many ways to help people. Match the "helping hands" with their descriptions.

- ♦ Work with a partner or a small group.
- ♦ Cut the cards and scramble them. Put them face down.
- ♦ Take turns. Turn over two cards and read them aloud.
- ♦ If the cards match, keep the cards.
- ♦ If the cards don't match, put them face down again. The next person takes a turn.
- ♦ Continue playing until all of the cards are matched.

✂ -

Dial-A-Ride	provides transportation for elderly or disabled people
Habitat for Humanity	builds low-cost housing
Public Action to Deliver Shelter	gives homeless people a place to sleep and food to eat
Mothers Against Drunk Driving	educates people about the dangers of drinking and driving
Meals for Seniors	delivers hot meals to the homes of elderly people
Alcoholics Anonymous	helps people stop drinking
Literacy Volunteers	teaches people to read and write English
Red Cross	provides food, clothing, and medical care during and after emergencies and disasters
United Way	raises money for other helping organizations
Adult Day Care	takes care of elderly people during the day

UNIT 23   THE GIFT

Katherine, Rosa, and Jamal are in the café. Katherine and Rosa are organizing things for a party.

Mr. Brashov arrives. "What a beautiful day," he says. Rosa says, "It's a very special day." Mr. Brashov is happy. He thinks Rosa remembered his birthday. But Rosa doesn't say, "Happy Birthday." She says, "Today is special because Jamal is going to fix the ice maker." Mr. Brashov is very sad. Nobody remembered his birthday.

A customer comes in the café. His name is Joe. Mr. Brashov hasn't seen Joe for awhile. Joe was at his son's cabin in the mountains. Joe shows Mr. Brashov some pictures. He tells Mr. Brashov to take a vacation.

Jamal is in the utility room. He is putting party decorations in his locker. Mr. Brashov walks in. Jamal tries to hide what he is doing. He doesn't want Mr. Brashov to know about the party. Fortunately, the phone rings. Mr. Brashov picks up the phone and says hello. But no one answers.

Joe comes back to the café with the keys to his son's cabin. He invites Mr. Brashov to the cabin. It's only two hours away. Mr. Brashov can go after work. When Katherine and Rose hear this, they are worried. If Mr. Brashov goes to the cabin, he will miss the surprise birthday party. Mr. Brashov leaves the café with Joe.

Jess and Katherine are in the utility room. Jess is typing a letter from the Internal Revenue Service (IRS) to give to Mr. Brashov. When Mr. Brashov returns to the café, Katherine gives him the mail.

Mr. Brashov sees a letter from the IRS. Someone from the IRS is coming to the café on Monday to see Mr. Brashov's tax records. Now Mr. Brashov cannot go to the cabin.

Jess has a solution to the problem. Mr. Brashov can call Emery Bradford to help him. If Emery and Mr. Brashov work on the tax records tonight, Mr. Brashov can go to the cabin on Saturday.

Emery comes to the café. Mr. Brashov is very depressed. This is not a very happy birthday for him. The phone rings again. It's Nicolae. He's calling to say "Happy Birthday" to his brother.

Mr. Brashov hangs up the phone. He calls information to get the number for the airport. He leaves the café. When Emery looks for Mr. Brashov, he can't find him. The door to the café opens. Everyone is there for Mr. Brashov's surprise party. But Mr. Brashov is not there!

Mr. Brashov is at the airport. His daughter, Anna, works at the ticket counter. She is very surprised to see her father. She hasn't seen him for a long time. Anna and Mr. Brashov talk.

Suddenly, Mr. Brashov sees his friends from the café. They want Mr. Brashov to return to the café for his surprise birthday party. Jess invites Anna to come, too, but she says she can't.

Back at the café, Mr. Brashov finally celebrates his birthday. There is a cake and gifts. And one gift is very special. Anna comes to the café—with her daughter, Elizabeth. For the first time, Mr. Brashov meets his granddaughter. Mr. Brashov finally has a very happy birthday.

ROLE-PLAY

HANDOUT 23-A

Mr. Brashov invited his employees to have dinner with him. They refused because they were going to have a surprise party for him. Practice making invitations.

- ♦ Work with a partner or in a small group.
- ♦ Write two more invitations on the blank cards.
- ♦ Cut the cards and scramble them. Put them face down in a pile.
- ♦ Take turns. Turn over a card and show it to a partner.
- ♦ Make invitations and accept or decline them using the examples in YOUR NEW LANGUAGE on page 132 of the *worktext*.

> EXAMPLE: *Go to a concert.*
> A: *Would you like to go to a jazz concert tomorrow night?*
> B: *I'm sorry, but I have to work tomorrow night.*
> A: *Well, maybe we can go another time.*
> B: *Sure. I'd like that.*

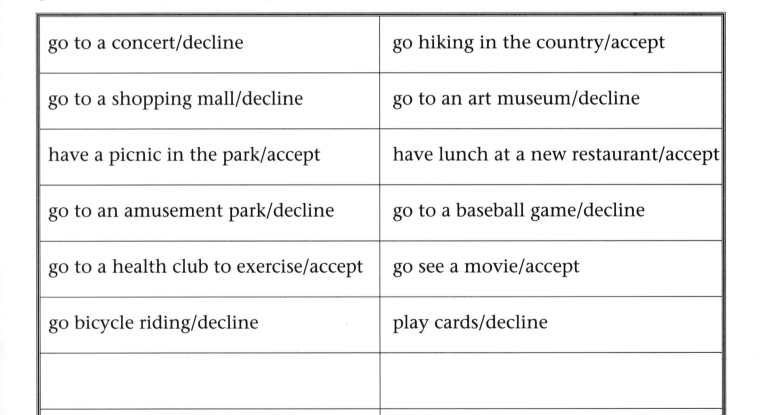

go to a concert/decline	go hiking in the country/accept
go to a shopping mall/decline	go to an art museum/decline
have a picnic in the park/accept	have lunch at a new restaurant/accept
go to an amusement park/decline	go to a baseball game/decline
go to a health club to exercise/accept	go see a movie/accept
go bicycle riding/decline	play cards/decline

DISCUSSION

HANDOUT 23-B

Mr. Brashov took a vacation at a cabin in the mountains. Where would you like to go on vacation? Read these six ads for vacations from a magazine.

- ◆ Work with a partner or in a small group.
- ◆ Choose the vacation ad that interests you the most.
- ◆ Work together to write questions and answers about the ad.
- ◆ Role-play a telephone call for information about the vacation place.
- ◆ Share the role-play with the class.

AD #1
Cruise the Mississippi
- houseboats
- 3-10 day cruises

call (800) 555-7742 for information

AD #2
Bike Tours
Name the state—
we'll make arrangements
Have fun & excercise too!
call (800) 111-2220

AD #3
Midwest Raft & Canoe Trips
- easy to advanced
- reasonable prices

call (800) 999-1231 for information

AD #4
Mall of America
- transportation
- lodging
- 1 meal deal

call (888) 778-4449

AD #5
Niagara Falls
- Maid of the Mist
- Cave of the Winds
- Museums
- Shopping

call (800) 741-0002

AD #6
Hike the Appalachians
- Camp, fish
- Bird watch
- Guide available

call Jim – (800) 928-5643

QUESTIONS	ANSWERS
1.	
2.	
3.	
4.	
5.	

PROBLEM-SOLVING

HANDOUT 23-C

Mr. Brashov's friends and employees have a big problem. They want to surprise Mr. Brashov.

- ♦ Work with a partner or in a small group.
- ♦ Cut the cards.
- ♦ Read the problems on the cards.
- ♦ Write one more problem.
- ♦ Choose one problem to discuss.
- ♦ Share your solutions with the class.

- -

PROBLEM #1   It is your first week at a new job. Tomorrow is one of your coworker's birthdays. You are asked to contribute $10.00 for a gift, card, and cake. You want your new co-workers to like you, but you are not comfortable giving $10.00 for a stranger's party.

SOLUTION:

PROBLEM #2   You gave a very expensive birthday gift to one of your friends. Now it is your birthday. But your friend doesn't give you a gift—only a card. You are very disappointed.

SOLUTION:

PROBLEM #3   A friend gave you a sweater for your birthday. It didn't fit, and you didn't like the color or style. You exchanged the sweater for a different one, but you didn't tell your friend. Your friend asks why you never wear the sweater.

SOLUTION:

PROBLEM #4   You have been invited to a surprise party for one of your neighbors. Your neighbor's husband tells you to bring a joke gift. You don't know what a joke gift is, and you are embarrassed to ask.

SOLUTION:

PROBLEM #5

SOLUTION:

COMPARE CULTURES

HANDOUT 23-D

Mr. Brashov worries about a letter from the Internal Revenue Service (IRS). Do you ever worry about taxes?

- Interview a partner about taxes.
- Ask the questions below or make up your own questions.
- Write your partner's answers on the lines.
- Share the interview with another pair.

NAME:	INTERVIEWER:
1. Is there a federal income tax in your native country?	
2. Do you think taxes in the United States are higher or lower than in your native country? Why or why not?	
3. How are taxes different in your native country than in the United States? How are taxes the same?	
4. What day are taxes due in your native country?	
5. Do you know anyone who has had tax problems? What happened?	
6. Do people in your native country pay city or state income taxes?	
7. What things should people pay taxes on?	
8. What things shouldn't people pay taxes on?	

Reproducible Handouts

UNIT 24 ALL'S WELL THAT ENDS WELL

It's snowing and Crossroads Café is closed. Jamal, Henry, Mr. Brashov, and Jess are looking at their watches. Rosa has a clipboard. She says to the men, "Let's synchronize our watches." Mr. Brashov and Rosa are having a dinner party for Katherine and Bill in four hours, forty-five minutes, and seventeen seconds. They are getting married tomorrow.

Everyone has a job to do except Henry. Mr. Brashov is making beef stroganoff. Jamal is putting up decorations. Carol is picking up the flowers.

A delivery man comes in the café with a box for Katherine. It's her wedding dress. Rosa opens the box to check on the dress. Oh no! The dress is the wrong size. It's huge. It's big enough for two or three Katherines to wear. Henry says, "Katherine had better start eating."

Henry goes outside to check the weather. It's snowing very hard. Rosa is worried about Katherine's grandfather. He is flying in from Europe, and someone has to pick him up at the airport.

There is another problem. Rosa hears Suzanne and David arguing in the kitchen. They were helping Rosa make pastries and Suzanne lost her mother's wedding ring!

Katherine and Bill enter the café. They are very happy. But when Katherine greets her children, Suzanne starts to cry and runs out of the room.

Everyone tells Katherine about the problems. Katherine is not happy any more. She asks about her wedding dress and decides to try it on. Katherine locks herself in the bathroom and cries after she sees the dress. She won't talk to anyone. She just cries.

Mr. Brashov tries to call the airport for information about flights from Europe. Everyone, except for Katherine, is listening to the radio. The weather is getting worse.

Finally, there is a job for Henry. Mr. Brashov decides to send Henry to the airport to pick up Katherine's grandfather. He gives Henry money for a taxi. Katherine gives Henry a description of her grandfather so Henry will recognize him.

Bill's family starts to arrive at the café for the dinner party. Bill's Uncle Antonio sees Rosa and calls her Katherine. He welcomes her to the family. Rosa is so surprised, she can't speak.

Henry has several problems at the airport. First, he picks up the wrong man. Then he finds the right man, but the taxi has a flat tire on the way back to Crossroads Café. Katherine's grandfather changes the tire.

Back at the café, Bill tells his family Rosa is not Katherine. Jamal says, "Katherine is at home. She's checking on her wedding dress." Bill's family doesn't know Katherine is in the utility room. She is a mess because she is crying.

Jamal helps Katherine climb out a window. Then she enters the café again— through the front door. Everyone is very happy to finally meet the bride!

The bride is happy, too. Her grandfather comes in with Henry and the taxi driver, and the party begins. When they all sit down to eat, Aunt Sophie finds the missing wedding ring in a pastry. All's well that ends well!

DIALOGUE

HANDOUT 24-A

Everyone at the café is getting ready for Bill and Katherine's party. What are they going to do?

♦ Work with a partner.
♦ Read the dialogue cards below.
♦ Cut the cards and scramble them. Put them face up.
♦ Put the dialogue cards in order while you watch the story clip.
♦ Share with another pair. Is the order of the cards the same?

- -

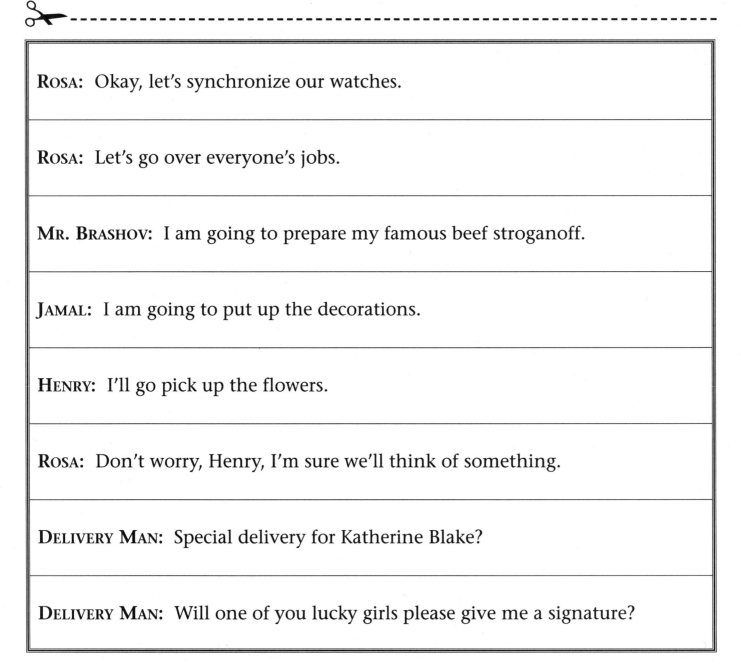

ROSA: Okay, let's synchronize our watches.

ROSA: Let's go over everyone's jobs.

MR. BRASHOV: I am going to prepare my famous beef stroganoff.

JAMAL: I am going to put up the decorations.

HENRY: I'll go pick up the flowers.

ROSA: Don't worry, Henry, I'm sure we'll think of something.

DELIVERY MAN: Special delivery for Katherine Blake?

DELIVERY MAN: Will one of you lucky girls please give me a signature?

ROLE-PLAY

HANDOUT 24-B

People use *going to* or *will* to talk about the future. What's in your future?

♦ Work with a partner.
♦ Each person writes a future expression and time on two blank cards.
♦ Cut the cards and scramble them. Put them face down in a pile.
♦ Take turns turning over the cards and role-play the situations.

> EXAMPLE: *going to/this afternoon*
> A: *What are you going to do this afternoon?*
> B: *I'm going to visit my aunt.*

♦ Share one role-play with the rest of the class.

✂ -

going to/this afternoon	going to/tomorrow morning
will/tomorrow night	will/ next week
going to/tonight	going to /next month
will/next winter	will /next spring
going to/next fall	going to/tomorrow afternoon
going to/tomorrow night	will/Saturday
will/on Sunday	will/in two weeks

MATCH UP

HANDOUT 24-C

What gifts did Bill and Katherine receive for their wedding? Think about the gifts people give on special occasions.

- ◆ Work with a partner or in a small group.
- ◆ Cut the cards and scramble them. Turn them face up.
- ◆ Match the gifts with the occasion.
- ◆ Share your cards with another pair or group. Are they the same or different?

✂ ---

crystal vase	housewarming
picture frame	new baby
silver comb and brush set	baby shower
bed sheets	wedding shower
$100.00	wedding gift
microwave oven	engagement gift
watch	high school graduation gift
car	college graduation
crystal table clock	10th anniversary

INTERVIEW

HANDOUT 24-D

Katherine and Bill are getting married.

- ◆ Interview someone about a wedding he or she attended.
- ◆ Ask the questions below, and add two more questions.
- ◆ Write the answers to the questions on the lines.
- ◆ Ask for permission to share the interview with the rest of the class.

NAME:	INTERVIEWER:
1. When was the last wedding you attended?	
2. Who were the bride and groom?	
3. How well did you know the bride and groom?	
4. Where was the wedding?	
5. What kind of dress did the bride wear? What did the groom wear?	
6. How many people were in the bridal party? What did they wear?	
7. How many people attended the wedding?	
8. Was there a reception (party)? What kind of food did you eat? Was there dancing?	
9. What gift did you give the bride and groom?	
10. Did you have fun at the wedding? Why or why not?	
11.	
12.	

UNIT 25 COMINGS AND GOINGS

Rosa is speaking Spanish to some customers. When Katherine comes to take their order, she speaks Spanish, too. Rosa says, "Congratulations. I almost understood you."

Jamal asks Katherine about her plans for the future. Katherine is leaving Crossroads Café to spend time with her children, help her husband, and go back to school. Katherine wants to be a lawyer. Rosa laughs and says, "That is a perfect job for you!"

Mr. Brashov has one last task for Katherine. He wants her to hire the new waitress. This worries Rosa.

Henry is in the office of a record producer, Danny. Henry wants to be a rock star. The producer listens to a tape of Henry and his band. They sound good, but the producer wants to hear them play in person. Henry invites Danny to a live concert at Crossroads Café.

The next day at the café, Jamal gets a phone call. It's a friend from Egypt. Jamal's friend, Abdullah, is in town and Jamal invites him for dinner.

Katherine interviews waitresses. She talks to many applicants, but she doesn't hire anyone. Rosa, Jess, and Mr. Brashov don't understand Katherine. There are many qualified people, but Katherine is still looking.

Jess wants to play chess with Mr. Brashov, but Mr. Brashov has too much work to do. He promises to play chess with Jess on Friday.

Henry tells Katherine about Danny. He is coming to Crossroads Café to hear Henry play. There's only one problem. Henry has to ask Mr. Brashov for permission to have a concert at the café. Mr. Brashov is not enthusiastic, but he agrees.

It's night. Jamal is eating dinner at home with Abdullah, his friend from Egypt. Abdullah's company needs a chief engineer. Abdullah offers Jamal a job in Egypt.

Jihan is surprised to learn Jamal wants to return to Egypt. Jihan likes her job, and she is happy in the United States. But Jamal is unhappy. He used to be an engineer, and now he is a handyman. Jamal doesn't want to be a handyman anymore.

The next day, Katherine interviews another applicant for the waitress job, a young Haitian woman, Marie. Rosa asks Katherine, "How was she?" Katherine answers, "Great." But Katherine didn't hire Marie. Katherine's looking for the perfect waitress.

Later in the evening, there is a crowd at the café. Danny, the producer, comes to hear Henry and the band. Henry is happy to see Danny there. But the next day, when he goes to see Danny, Henry is very disappointed. Danny doesn't think Henry is good enough to sign a contract. Danny tells Henry to go to college.

It's Katherine's last day at Crossroads Café. And surprise—the café finally has a new waitress—Marie. Katherine introduces Jess to Marie. Then Jess and Mr. Brashov start to play chess. A delivery man interrupts their game. Jess is disappointed. Mr. Brashov promises to finish the game after Katherine's party.

The café is closed for the day, and the party for Katherine begins. Everyone is there except Carol and Jess. Then the phone rings. It's Carol. She has terrible news. Jess was in a car accident. Jess is dead. Katherine's party is over.

TALK ABOUT THE FUTURE

HANDOUT 25-A

Katherine is planning to go back to college. Jamal and Jihan are planning to return to Egypt. Think about your plans for the future.

♦ Work with a partner.
♦ Fill in the boxes with information about your plans for the future.
♦ Share the information with another pair or the class.

Both of us are definitely planning to . . .	A might . . .
B might . . .	Neither of us is planning to . . .

PROBLEM-SOLVING

HANDOUT 25-B

Katherine is going back to college. In addition to taking college classes, many adults take classes at other places such as park districts or community centers.

♦ Work with a partner or in a small group.
♦ Read the class descriptions below.
♦ Decide which classes each of the Crossroads Café characters might take.
♦ Give your reasons why the character would take the class.
♦ Choose one class you might be interested in and give your reasons.
♦ Share your choices and reasons with the class.

Cooking Around the World This class will teach you how to make a five-course meal from a country on every one of the seven continents. Tuesday: 7:00–10:00 P.M. Five weeks beginning 10/14 $65.00	**Advanced Guitar** Improve your technique and write music in this fast-paced class. The instructor is a professional who has played guitar in several well-known bands. Wednesday: 8:00–9:30 P.M. 10 weeks beginning 10/15 $100.00
Financial Planning for Retirement Now is the perfect time to plan your retirement. Will you have enough money to do what you want? How much money will you need? What kind of health insurance do you need? These and other questions will be answered in this class. Monday: 6:30–8:30 P.M. Four weeks beginning 10/13 $55.00	**Step-Parenting** Marriage is hard work, especially if you have stepchildren. Learn how to avoid problems with stepchildren and develop healthy, loving relationships with them. Thursday: 7:00–8:30 P.M. Three weeks beginning 11/16 $30.00
Tips for Running a Successful Business Want to own your own business or just thinking about it? Chances are you don't know everything you need to know. Get advice from a trio of successful businessmen and women. You'll save time and money! Wednesday: 7:00–9:00 P.M. Five weeks beginning 11/1 $65.00	**Study Skills for Adults** Is returning to school in your future? Learn how to manage your time effectively, organize class notes, use the Internet to do research, and review for tests. Thursday: 8:00–9:30 P.M. Four weeks beginning 11/2 $40.00

INTERVIEW

HANDOUT 25-C

What's going to happen to the people at Crossroads Café?

- ◆ Read the questions.
- ◆ Check YES or NO for each question.
- ◆ Write two more questions in the blanks.
- ◆ Compare your answers with a partner. Are your answers the same or different? Give reasons for your answers.
- ◆ Share your answers with the class.

	YES	NO
1. Is Mr. Brashov going to slow down?		
2. Is Henry planning to go to college?		
3. Is Henry going to be a famous rock star some day?		
4. Is Mr. Brashov going to get a new chess partner?		
5. Is Jamal going to go back to Egypt?		
6. Is Jihan going to be happy in Egypt?		
7. Is Katherine going to be a lawyer?		
8. Is Henry going to give any more concerts at Crossroads Café?		
9. Will Rosa and Marie become friends?		
10. Will Katherine and Rosa remain friends?		
11.		
12.		

REASONS

HANDOUT 25-D

Millions of people come to the United States each year. Many stay here. Some, like Jamal and Jihan, return to their native countries. Think about why some people stay and other people leave.

- ♦ Work with a partner or in a small group.
- ♦ Read the cards.
- ♦ Each partner adds *one reason for* **staying** and *one reason for* **returning** home.
- ♦ Cut the cards and scramble them.
- ♦ Discuss the cards and put them in two columns: *reasons for* **staying** *in the United States* and *reasons for* **returning** *home.*
- ♦ Share your answers with the class.

✂ -

a good job	cost of living
educational opportunities	medical care
chance to own a business	friends and family
high level of technology	own property
war in native country	crime
variety of people	culture
freedom of religion	language
spouse and children are citizens	government

WINDS OF CHANGE

It's early afternoon at Crossroads Café, and Mr. Brashov is thinking about Jess. Mr. Brashov misses Jess a lot.

Jihan comes in the café to see Jamal. Jihan tells Jamal, "I have found a company to ship our things to Egypt." Jamal surprises Jihan when he says, "I don't think we should move back to Egypt." They discuss their decision to return to Egypt, and finally, Jihan agrees with Jamal. They will stay in the United States.

Carol Washington is at home with her son, Daryl. Someone knocks at the door. It's Mr. Brashov. He is holding a shopping bag. Mr. Brashov has something for Carol. It's a chess board—the one he and Jess used to play chess.

Carol shows Mr. Brashov an envelope with tickets for a cruise to the Greek Islands. She wanted to surprise Jess on their anniversary, but now Jess is gone. When Mr. Brashov leaves, Carol cries.

Katherine makes a surprise visit to the café. She shows Rosa a catalogue from City College. Henry stops working to talk to Katherine, too. But Marie tells him to get back to work.

A few minutes later, Henry has an accident. His hand is bleeding. While Marie helps Henry, Katherine waits on the customers. Henry tells Marie, "You should have been a nurse." Marie tells Henry, "I am."

Marie was a nurse in Haiti. She has to go back to school before she can be a nurse in the United States. Henry doesn't like to talk about going to school. He wants to be a rock star, not a student. Marie advises Henry to go to college.

Carol Washington comes in the café to talk to Mr. Brashov. This time Carol has something for Mr. Brashov. She gives him the tickets for the cruise to the Greek Islands. At first, Mr. Brashov doesn't want to accept the tickets. But finally he takes them—for Jess.

A few days later, Mr. Brashov walks around the café with a businessman, Mr. Clayborne. When Mr. Clayborne leaves, Mr. Brashov surprises everyone. He tells them "Mr. Clayborne is the new owner of Crossroads Café. I am 65-years old, and I want to enjoy my life."

It's a week later. The café is closed, but Mr. Brashov and Mr. Clayborne are talking. Jamal comes in with a box and news for Mr. Brashov. He and Jihan changed their minds again. This time they have definitely decided to return to Egypt. Mr. Clayborne also has news for Mr. Brashov. He will bring his own employees to Crossroads Café.

Jamal stops to talk to Henry, Rosa, and Marie. Henry has some news, too. He is going to go to college. Jamal congratulates Henry.

A few minutes later, Mr. Brashov says good-bye to Mr. Clayborne. Now it is Mr. Brashov's turn to give Rosa some news. Mr. Clayborne is not going to be the owner of Crossroads Café. Mr. Brashov has decided to keep the café and hire a manager. The new manager is Rosa Rivera!

ROLE-PLAY

HANDOUT 26-A

Before they go to Egypt, Jamal and Jihan have many things to do.

♦ Work with a partner or in a small group.
♦ Read the cards below. Each person writes one or two more things to do on the blank cards.
♦ Cut the cards and scramble them. Put them face down in a pile.
♦ Take turns. Turn over a card. Read the card and say three things you have to do about the topic. Use **have to** and **must**.
♦ Add one more thing to your partner's list.

EXAMPLE: *Wash dishes*
        A: *You have to turn on the hot water.*
            You must add soap to the water.
            You have to put the dirty dishes in the sink.
        B: *You must close the drain.*

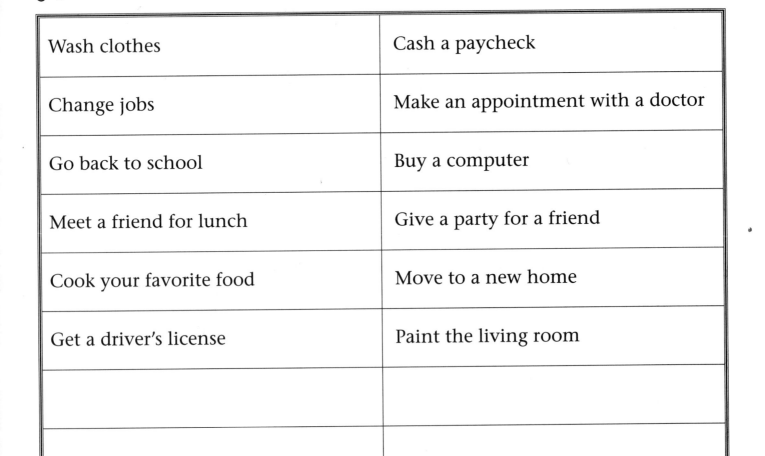

Wash clothes	Cash a paycheck
Change jobs	Make an appointment with a doctor
Go back to school	Buy a computer
Meet a friend for lunch	Give a party for a friend
Cook your favorite food	Move to a new home
Get a driver's license	Paint the living room

INFORMATION GAP

HANDOUT 26-B

Look at this map of a college campus.

A

♦ Work with a partner.

♦ Ask questions to find these places: Classroom Building, Arts Building, Tennis Courts, Parking Lot 7, Parking Lot 8, and Law School.

> EXAMPLE: A: *Where's the <u>Classroom Building</u>?*
> B: *It's <u>in the middle of the campus</u>.*

♦ Write the information on the map.

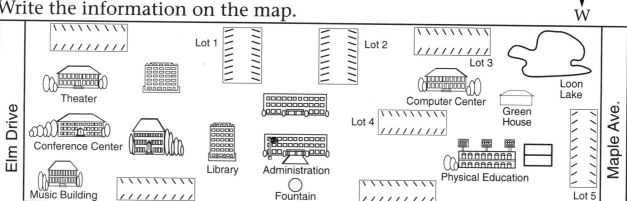

Look at this map of a college campus.

B

♦ Work with a partner.

♦ Ask questions to find these places: Music Building, Library, Administration Building, Computer Center, Physical Education, and Parking lot 6.

> EXAMPLE: B: *Where's the <u>Music Building</u>?*
> A: *It's across from the <u>Conference Center</u>.*

♦ Write the information on the map.

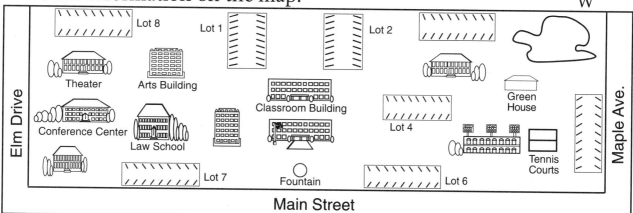

DIALOGUE

HANDOUT 26-C

Carol Washington comes to Crossroads Café to talk to Mr. Brashov. What do they talk about?

Work with a partner.
Read the dialogue cards below.
Put the conversation in order while you watch the video.
Share with another pair. Is the order of the cards the same?

✂ -

ALL: Hi. How are you doing, Carol?
CAROL: But I'd like to talk to you, Victor, if you've got a minute.
MR. BRASHOV: Why don't we step into my office?
MARIE: Thanks for helping out, Katherine.
MR. BRASHOV: I know exactly what you mean.
CAROL: Victor, there's something I'd like you to have.
MR. BRASHOV: Carol . . . I can't take these.
CAROL: I couldn't possibly take this trip.
CAROL: This would make him very happy.
CAROL: Don't wait for the perfect time to do anything.

INTERVIEW

HANDOUT 26-D

Think about Edgar Villarmarin's life in the United States. Is your life similar or different?

- ◆ Interview a partner about his or her life in the United States.
- ◆ Ask the questions below.
- ◆ Add two more questions.
- ◆ Write the answers in the chart.
- ◆ Share the interview with another pair or the class.

NAME:	INTERVIEWER:
1. When did you come to the United States?	
2. How old were you?	
3. What did you do first (go to school, get a job)?	
4. Did you have any goals? What were they?	
5. Have you achieved any of your goals? Which ones?	
6. Do you have any new goals? What are they?	
7. How will you achieve your new goals?	
8. What advice do you have for newcomers to the United States?	
9.	
10.	